SOWING WILD OATS

*Fifth in the Series of Stories About Growing Up
in and Around Small Towns in the Midwest*

Edited by

Jean Tennant

Shapato Publishing, LLC
Everly, Iowa

Published by: Shapato Publishing, LLC
                 PO Box 476
                 Everly, Iowa 51338

ISBN: 978-0615726380
Library of Congress Control Number: 2012921097

First Printing November 2012

Interior sketches by LaVonne M. Hansen

Photo provided by Karen Howard

INTRODUCTION

With this being the fifth year of the Midwest anthologies, the number of quality stories coming our way has, naturally, increased. While it's been a luxury to have so many good stories to choose from, it's also been harder than ever to choose which ones will go into this latest book. But choose I finally did, and I'm pleased that *Sowing Wild Oats* contains thirty-two wonderful stories and one poem by authors both familiar and new.

As always, this couldn't have been put together without the help of others. Gathering stories, sorting through the hundreds of submissions and making difficult decisions isn't the end of it. Editing is also a big part of the process. Stories aren't chosen just on the basis of how well written they are—though that is, of course, an added bonus—but rather on if they have a universal appeal and if they're likely to touch the hearts of readers. As a result, first-time authors submitted many of the stories chosen, and often these required a fair amount of editing.

And this is where I have to be honest—these anthologies would be dead in the water without the editing help of my good friend and fellow author, Betty Taylor. A retired schoolteacher, tireless researcher and native Midwesterner, Betty has more than once saved me, a city girl, from making some embarrassing mistakes. But best of all, I can always count on her to make me laugh.

I also must thank artist LaVonne Hansen, of Hartley, Iowa, who has provided the wonderful sketches included in the anthologies since the very first one. Her art has done much to enhance the pages of the books.

We hope you enjoy the stories contained within these covers. If you'd like to submit something for next year's anthology, tentatively titled *Needle in a Haystack*, submission guidelines are listed at the end of this book.

Jean Tennant
Shapato Publishing, LLC
Everly, Iowa

Sketch by LaVonne M. Hansen

TABLE OF CONTENTS

Sowing Wild Oats

MOONSHINE IN THE ATTIC

Tom Phillips

In later years, when my Uncle Robert spoke of the great explosion, he almost always began by saying what a pleasant, tranquil day it had been up until that time. He *thought* it had all happened on a lazy Sunday afternoon, though with the passing of time he admitted he was no longer totally sure about the day.

The chaos occurred as the family was lounging downstairs in the two-story frame house in northeastern Nebraska. My aunt and uncle had a houseguest at the time. Uncle Robert's mother, my grandmother, had come to spend a few days with them.

I never knew this grandmother. She passed on a mere two weeks after I was born—and, despite what my older brother told me repeatedly as I grew up, the two events were not related—but the description that has come down from those who knew her all portray her as a quiet, somewhat prim, devout lady.

My uncle was not quiet, prim, *or* devout. He was a card-playing, sometimes hell-raiser who was known to occasionally imbibe.

Midway through the Prohibition Era, he could no longer tolerate the thirst. Like many others throughout the country who used sheds, outbuildings, cellars, and hidden places by the creek to brew their own, my uncle also had some private action going

1

with a homemade still. Only in his case, he put the still in the attic.

He had carefully smuggled in and installed the equipment in the small garret right under the roof of the modest house. Three large batches of hooch were continually brewing in barrels that took up most of the available space.

He was pleased with his decision. The attic was convenient, secluded, and most importantly, he didn't have far to go to quench his thirst. All seemed well with the world. Except that my uncle hadn't allowed for the heat of the Nebraska summer beating through the uninsulated roof. There was no way to cool the space—it would be years before electricity reached the rural areas—so the only thing that stood between Uncle Robert's moonshine and the glaring sun was the roof with its weather-worn shingles.

As the family went quietly about their daily routines downstairs, the yeast and the sugar and the alcohol were fermenting upstairs.

Eventually, it was all too much. About mid-afternoon Uncle Robert's formula reached critical mass.

Three enormous explosions rocked the house.

WHAM! WHAM! WHAM!

Like cannons fired in salvo, the concussions tore the tops off the barrels. The lids blew straight up into the ceiling in the attic, bounced off and ricocheted around the small room.

The story was likely embellished as the years went by, but in some versions wisps of powdery plaster fell from the downstairs ceilings and maybe even a saltshaker tipped over on the kitchen table.

Pandemonium reigned throughout the house. Uncle Robert, of course, knew immediately what had happened. But even before he could go to check on the damage, he had another, immediate problem to deal with, which was how to explain the noise to his mother, who called from the parlor, demanding to know what was going on.

My uncle's accounts of what he told her varied a bit over the years, but apparently they shifted first from "Must be some thunder in the distance," to a more believable explanation that had something to do with limbs falling on the roof from the dead oak tree next to the house, accompanied by, "I should have cut that thing down years ago."

Eventually, after calming his mother, he ran to the attic. There he encountered a scene of destruction. The lids of the barrels were mangled and scattered from corner to corner. The blasts hadn't blown holes in the roof, but they had knocked some shingles loose. Support beams in the attic were chipped and gouged where the lids had struck them as they flew around the room. The barrels had tipped over and their contents were flowing over the floor and down the steps.

As unobtrusively as he could, so as not to arouse his mother's suspicions, he used every available towel, washcloth, sheet, and bedspread in the house to sop up the residue, which was now oozing its way down the attic steps.

Some of the stuff even worked its way through the plaster and later there were several spots visible on the ceiling. I'm guessing my uncle probably attributed those to water seeping through the holes in the roof caused by that miserable oak tree.

I don't know how he might have accounted for any odor that surely must have lingered, or why the next few days had to be spent washing every piece of linen in the house.

But I'm pretty sure my uncle would have found a way to explain it.

Tom Phillips grew up on a farm near Lincoln, Nebraska. After thirty-six years in the military, during which he led a unit through a terrorist escape, served in Operation Desert Storm, and led some of the first American troops into Sarajevo, he worked as a university administrator before beginning a full-time career writing about Americana, military and defense issues, and baseball.

STILL CRAZY IN IOWA

Mark Smith

Running a still isn't a hobby associated with an Iowa farm. Usually one envisions this activity high in the mountains of Tennessee. But for a few weeks in the mid-seventies, a cottage industry on our farm produced gallons of prime brew. Until its tragic demise.

Dad loved a good auction. There was no telling what treasures he could find at one. Half a saddle, a dozen horse collars with the accompanying harness, a horse drawn mower—all items he had picked up at one sale or another. But it was the bottle capper he brought home that caused the most trouble.

He opened the trunk of his car after one of these auctions to display his most recent find: an old rusty bottle capper with a box of virgin caps. In the back seat were three boxes of dusty old bottles and some gallon jugs.

"What have you gotten now?" Mom asked.

Dad answered, "I've decided that instead of buying pop for the boys we can save money by making our own root beer."

We boys were overcome with amazement. A vision of all-you-can-drink root beer filled our minds. Mom, however, had survived several of Dad's schemes and reacted accordingly. "Do you know how to make root beer?" she asked.

Dad reached into his pocket and pulled out a small box. "All I have to do is follow the directions. We're going to save a ton of money."

As it turned out, making root beer isn't all that hard.

First, take a trashcan (newly bought for this purpose) to act as the "still," and wash it thoroughly with soap and water, then rinse it again to get rid of any remaining soap residue. The bottles are washed, as is the funnel (also bought expressly for the root beer) and as the bottles dry, measure five gallons of water into the trashcan. Add an obscene amount of sugar, along with a few spoons of brewer's yeast. Then, and only then, add a small bottle of root beer extract to the mix.

Stir the viscous brew with a new spatula (bought especially for . . . never mind, you get the point) until the sugar is dissolved.

Siphon the syrupy mess into the bottles and cap them. According to the instructions, completely filling the bottles is bad, because then the yeast wouldn't have enough oxygen to multiply and carbonate the root beer. So Dad left a couple of inches of air at the top of each one.

Five gallons is a lot of root beer, however, and Dad ran out of containers before he ran out of root beer. Undaunted, he took a couple of gallon milk jugs, cleaned and filled them, as well. Then he boxed up all of the containers and transported them to the basement to brew.

Now came the hard part—waiting. For two weeks my brothers and I checked the bottles daily. The glass ones remained blissfully undisturbed, but the milk jugs puffed out like balloons and hissed at the caps. Dad wound some tape around the necks of the jugs and the hissing ceased.

Finally, the great day arrived. We carried the root beer upstairs to be sampled. The milk jugs seemed to have deflated a bit, but the glass ones were pristine with their shiny brass-colored caps. Dad took one of the milk jugs and carefully unwound the tape. He slowly unscrewed the lid. A faint hissing was heard and the slightest vapor rose from the mouth of the jug.

Dad poured himself a glass and tasted it. "Not bad," he said. "Not bad at all."

As oldest, I was next. I grabbed a glass bottle and used my pocketknife to pop the shiny brass cap. Maybe I shook it. Maybe a couple of inches of air had allowed the yeast to over-carbonate.

But for whatever reason, I found myself clutching a root beer geyser. Light brown foam roared forth, rising halfway to the kitchen ceiling, falling slightly and then renewing itself to reach for ever greater heights. I stared in amazement for perhaps ten seconds, first at the geyser, then at the near-empty bottle in my hands. All that soaring root beer had to go somewhere, and somewhere was all over Mom's kitchen.

Dad quickly organized a cleanup crew. A new tablecloth was found and the table and floor were quickly wiped free of the sticky substance.

Dad decided he would use the gallon milk jugs for his future brewing needs, losing interest in the capped bottles.

We boys, on the other hand, after several failed attempts to sample the contents, discovered their potential as water—or rather, root beer—cannons. A single nail hole in the cap made a bottle good for five minutes of chasing a brother around the farm and giving him a sticky shower (soon to be followed by a real one) if we got close enough. Mom was kind enough to overlook such monkeyshines as long as they took place outdoors. She would just sigh and throw our soaked clothing into the washing machine we kept on the enclosed front porch.

Dad's second batch went well, and it went quickly. Three boys could drink a lot of root beer. By the third batch in as many weeks he became annoyed at the fruits of his labor being consumed so quickly, and became "too busy" to make another batch.

No matter. The root beer maker's apprentice had paid close attention to Dad's methods and felt confident he could duplicate the process.

I washed the trashcan and funnel, wiped the spatula, and started washing the containers. Not just the milk jugs, though. I wanted *my* root beer to be fizzy, so I washed out the glass gallon jugs Dad had brought home from the auction, because I was sure their screw tops wouldn't let the gas escape like the milk jugs' had. Further, I put an extra spoon of brewer's yeast into the vat before I mixed it.

After siphoning the brew into the glass jugs, I screwed the lids down tight and stored them beside the washer in the porch. The sight of the five glass jugs sitting on the cement floor gave me a happy feeling, knowing that in a week my work would be complete.

Five days later an explosion went off on the porch. I was watching TV at the time, a police show, and thought it was part of the program. But none of the actors responded to the sound. So, at the commercial, I went to the porch to investigate, and found myself facing carnage.

One of the glass jugs had exploded, wiping out its neighbors. Five gallons of root beer had flooded across the cement floor around the washer. Saddened, I swept up the broken glass and wiped the mess with a towel.

The next morning, as Mom was carrying a load of dirty clothes to the washer, she noticed a large number of flies crawling on the floor. She soon discovered why. As she crossed the porch, the floor made a squelching noise and something sticky pulled her shoes off her feet. Past experience left her with no doubt as to a course of action.

"Mark!" she shouted, "why is the floor sticky?"

"I don't know," I answered.

"Did you spill some of your root beer?" Mom looked again. "Where *is* your root beer . . . ?"

"Oh, one of the jugs exploded. I cleaned it up."

It says something about both my childhood and my mom that the news of an explosion in her house did not faze her.

"How much root beer did you spill?"

"Five gallons."

"Five gallons of root beer?" she cried. "No wonder the floor is sticky. Mop it up NOW!"

There was no explaining things to Mom, so I mopped the floor and waited for it to dry.

Squelch, squelch.

I mopped it again.

Squelch, squelch.

A third time.

"Mark, the floor is still sticky!"

After being mopped four times the floor stopped grabbing people's shoes; after six times it stopped making noises.

Mom banned all future brewing efforts and for as long as we owned the farm we boys lamented the loss of our still.

But every summer, the flies continued to settle on the cement floor where it had been.

Mark Smith grew up in rural Iowa, in a family of seven. His formative years were filled with adventures involving animals (wild and domestic), snow, firearms, the odd explosion or two, and way too much work. He insists that he has flashbacks as a result of his upbringing. His family chooses to refer to them as "daydreams." He has been published in several anthologies, a national magazine, and is the author of *Storm*, a children's book.

Clara Mugge
Sketch by Nancy Roth

FOR BETTER OR FOR WORSE

Betty Hembd Taylor

Rain clouds threatened the outdoor wedding behind my sister-in-law's house in Sioux City.

"What's the alternate plan?" I asked the mother of the bride as she met us at the car. "There is no alternate plan," she giggled nervously. "I asked God to hold off on the rain until after four o' clock.

Prenuptial music intruded on my ears from a sound system in the back yard. Hard Rock! I looked at the vehicles that had brought the wedding guests. Half of the crowd came in cars and the other half came on Harleys. Cindy was about to marry a motorcycle mechanic.

I had never seen Dale in anything other than blue jeans and a leather jacket, so I was a bit curious to see him in his wedding finery. The warm summer afternoon decreed that the leather jacket would not be part of his attire, but I was bit surprised to see him in his blue jeans and a denim shirt with cut out sleeves and a frayed collar.

Nancy and Cathy, sisters of the bride, mingled with the guests on the lawn. Cathy went to the groom and combed his long, curly hair with a yellow hair pick. Smiling and slightly embarrassed he submitted to the unfamiliar ordeal. Her best effort on the hair was some improvement and Dale looked better groomed than I had ever seen him

Guests continued to arrive. Half of the crowd wore conventional middle-class clothing and the other half wore denim.

His friends mingled with each other and we mingled with those dressed in polyester suits and dresses. Each group cast uncomfortable glances at the other. One of Dale's friends wore a Harley cap and a faded denim vest to match his blue jeans. Words on the shirt were partially obscured by the vest, but the picture of a semi and the letters U-C-K were visible.

Orv leaned toward me and in a quiet voice said, "I hope there's a T-R in front of those letters."

We chuckled and turned our attention to my nephews, Cindy's brothers. They were dressed in three-piece suits and proudly showed off their families, while we conversed easily. This diverse group belongs to my brother Gordon, now deceased, and will always remain special to me.

I spoke to the maternal grandmother, who was gracious in any situation. Having long since learned to look beneath the external and not prejudge a situation, she moved easily from one group to the other, visiting with all the guests.

Soon a very conventional minister appeared. He positioned himself under a conventional flower-covered arch. The rock music stopped and the strains of *Lohengrin's Wedding March* filled the air. The guy with the writing on the T-shirt was to be the best man. He tossed his cap lightly to one of the denim-clad girls, smoothed his hair with his hands, and took his place beside the groom.

Nancy and Cathy emerged from the house wearing raspberry-colored bridesmaid's dresses and carrying flowers. Half of the wedding party was traditional and the other half wore blue jeans.

I hardly dared to guess what Cindy might be wearing, but then she appeared in a modest long white dress with an accordion pleated skirt, flowers in her hair, six-months pregnant, and barefoot.

I always think of my serious, proper mother when I am in an unusual situation, and I wondered how she would have reacted if she had lived to see this day. The maternal grandmother, aged 83, sat serenely a few rows ahead of us. Neither her hair nor her dignity was out of place and she was wearing a plum-colored dress.

Leaning toward my husband, I whispered, "If Clara Mugge can act like this is a normal situation, I guess I can too."

The traditional pastor held a traditional service right down to ". . . love, honor, and cherish . . ." and ". . . If anyone can show just cause why this couple . . . "and then it was time for the reception. Half of the crowd sat to the left and the other half sat to the right.

The mother of the bride, a school teacher, laid out a lovely table with a beautifully arranged ham and cheese plate, fruit, punch, coffee, and a three-tiered cake. She had learned to love this new son-in-law, and she shared the happiness of the young couple. It was evident that her prayers had been answered as the sky cleared and tensions eased.

The suit and polyester crowd carried on typical after wedding conversations. Orv and my brother-in-law made a few comments about something my sister and I had not noticed. The denim-clad cake cutter had a flower tattooed in her cleavage. To this day, when Orv tells the story he always adds, "And the rose was growing."

Later the bride and groom roared away on their Harley, decorated with traditional wedding decorations and trailing a line of shoes. Half of the crowd roared after them and the other half stayed on the lawn

I didn't see Cindy and Dale again until several months later—at Clara Mugge's funeral. She lay serenely in her casket. Neither her hair nor her dignity was out of place, and she was wearing a plum-colored dress.

Cindy and Dale returned the respect she'd shown to them at the wedding with respect for her at the funeral. Cindy was wearing a dress and shoes, and Dale, dressed in a three-piece suit, proudly carried his baby daughter in his arms.

Betty Hembd Taylor's roots are embedded in Northwest Iowa soil. Her extended family includes a myriad of unique individuals who nourish her soul and provide substance for her stories.

Photo provided by Carolyn Rohrbaugh

THE LOVE OF MUD SQUISHING BETWEEN MY TOES

Carolyn Rohrbaugh

Spring rain was always a time of great happiness to me when I was a little girl. There was nothing I enjoyed more than going barefoot before the ground was even warm. I would beg Mother to let me take my shoes off and run free, to feel the grass tickling my feet and mud squishing between my toes. I begged, "Please, let me take off my shoes." But her answer was always the same: "Not until the ground warms up."

And, even though it was spring, Mother still bundled us in head scarves, winter coats and overshoes to walk the three blocks to school.

One of our neighbors, known to everyone as "Grandma Hill," had a large garden beside the street that was on our way to school. The snow was melting, and the black soil of her garden space made me long to walk in the mud and squish it between my toes. It was too much for me to resist. I childishly thought my boots would protect my shoes and I'd still be able to feel the soft mud around my feet.

Mesmerized, I headed toward the garden. My sister, Darla Rae, stared in disbelief.

With each step I sank deeper, and soon I realized this wasn't quite as delightful as I thought it would be. The mud tugged and sucked my boot deeper and deeper. As I tried to pull it from the quagmire my foot slid from the overshoe, then a shoe and then a sock. By then I was crying, Darla had deserted me, and I didn't know how I would escape from this not-so-glamorous trap.

Another neighbor, Mrs. Loaf, lived across the street from Grandma Hill's garden. We had always thought she was a crabby lady, but through my tears I saw Mrs. Loaf plowing into the mud to rescue me. She retrieved my boot, shoe and sock, took me across the street to her house, where she cleaned me up before sending me on my way to school.

I thought Mother would never know, but Mrs. Loaf called her and I was scolded when I arrived home later that day.

The scolding didn't help, as a few days later I couldn't resist the lure of Grandma Hill's garden again, and I waded into the mud with the same results and a very kind and patient Mrs. Loaf once more helping me out.

We were never spanked by our parents, but Mother was very firm. "It better not happen again," she warned.

But only a short while later, one Sunday morning as Darla and I walked home from Sunday school, I was again tempted by the mud puddles created by the previous night's rain.

We had decided to take a short cut home, past the baseball diamond. I was so proud to be wearing my new store-bought skirt. Mother always made our clothes, so a store-bought skirt was something special, but there was that baseball diamond, with all that wonderful, squishy mud.

Good shoes, store-bought skirt and all, I strutted into that muddy baseball diamond. I knew I was in big trouble when I fell in face-first, covering my beautiful skirt with gunk.

My sister was crying, "You're really in trouble this time."

The town bully lived a few houses away, and as I looked up I saw him coming toward us.

Darla yelled, "Get up, here comes Ronny, we need to run!"

I was in kindergarten, Darla was in second grade, Ronny was in junior high—and we were afraid of him. Quickly pulling my shoes and socks from the mud, we ran as fast as we could toward home, where I would have to face our parents one more time.

Thus ended my fascination with muddy gardens and baseball diamonds. After that I settled for the grass tickling my feet and just the memory of mud squishing between my toes.

Carolyn Rohrbaugh enjoys basing her writing on true stories. In 2011 Carolyn and her husband, Bill, traveled to California where they saw a mother gray whale and her baby in the Klamath, California River. This encounter inspired her to write a children's book, *Mama & Asha*, which was published by Shapato Publishing and released in March of 2012. She enjoys traveling, gardening and most of all her family.

KNOT UNUSUAL

Jim Davis

During my youth on the farm, threshing was the big event of the year. Still, I was able to ride the binder, and even help shock oats, long before I felt a part of threshing time, much less of the threshing crew—long before I did not have to wait at the end of the lunch line.

Threshing, though on its way out and yielding to the combine when I was growing up in the 'fifties, was spectacular. A menagerie of men, tractors, and teams of horses and mules milled around a huge diesel engine attached by a foot-wide black belt to the clattering gray threshing machine. ("Thrashin" was closer to what we said, and to what it did.) The owner, who farmed on a larger scale than most in the area, took it from farm to farm, outward from his own place. Neighbors would trade work, so relatively little money ever changed hands despite all the labor involved. My first work for others was to pay our debt, not for my own spending money.

Teams and wagons, or occasionally tractors and wagons, paraded between a farmer's fields and the thresher. Always stationed at a carefully selected place, it built an enormous pile of golden, fragrant straw—almost always oat straw on our farm. Our Percheron mares loved the grain, and ate it more daintily than they did ears of corn in their stable feed boxes.

A growing boy, however, faced a clear hierarchy on the threshing crew, and water boy, even with the advantage of a Shetland pony, just didn't count. The top, unchallenged spot, of course, was held by the man who owned and operated the thresher. Nearly as remote, and more enviable, were the stackers. These men could place bundled grain on the wagon so well that the load was never lost despite the steep slopes and rocky terrain of the Ozarks. They appeared tireless and rode their wagons to the thresher where, high on the load of grain, they pitched bundles into the gray maw of the machine. Never straining to lift themselves, they always took the load down as evenly balanced as they had built it. They even seemed to handle easily the wild-eyed young horses, the green teams, pitching and bolting to avoid the din of the thresher. Most of the stackers were older, intimate members of an adult male community. The best of them were called when bundled grain was to be stacked outside for the winter. That art was beyond aspiration.

Pitchers were next in line. They threw bundled grain onto the wagons, which primarily required "main strength and awkwardness." But a good pitcher I would soon learn put each bundle just where the stacker could most easily grab it and place it in the load. A poor pitcher increased the stacker's work ten-fold; a foolish one tried to "cover him up" by throwing bundles faster than the stacker could place them. Either gained as little regard as he showed good sense.

Entry into the threshing crew, however, came as a sacker. The sackers worked right next to the machine, in the din and the dust, and caught the grain as it poured from a dual-sided spout into large burlap bags we called "gunny-sacks." When one sack was full, the sacker threw a lever to channel grain into the other sack hanging from the other side of the spout. Before it was filled, the full one was tied, stacked to one side, and a new sack was fitted over the spout so the lever could be reversed with no loss of grain.

Precision, speed and strength—all were required to join the crew. Oh, how I wanted to learn to tie that miller's knot and become just as grimy a "field hand" as everyone else.

"Gather the top of the sack tightly in your left hand; whip the precut piece of twine around the top, lacing it over your third finger but under all the rest; wrap it twice more; catch the final

20

wrap with your third finger and pull it through; jerk both ends tight and the sack is tied." Over and over I practiced.

Long after I made the crew, moved to pitcher, and even learned to stack, I still tie the miller's knot automatically. Actually, Thursday morning's trash or a bag of autumn leaves just seems less onerous if I secure it with a miller's knot.

Jim Davis directs the Iowa Writing Project and teaches English at UNI. He has been an educator since 1966, in Iowa since 1973.

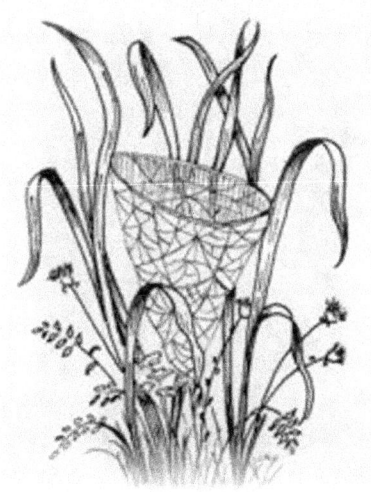

FIRST DAY ON THE JOB

Robert G. Sherman

September 8, 1968 . . . the first day of my thirteenth year, it was. A perplexing day I had been waiting for with manly anticipation. Finally, I had reached the threshold on the working world. Yes, I had held past positions such as lemonade stand vendor, golf caddy and lawn boy, to name a few, but on this day I was going to work with my dad and the other men on the crew. We were roofers.

A small town in South Dakota needed a new roof on their very tall church. Normally work began soon after sunrise, but that morning we started late. A few days earlier a teenage girl had been killed in a fireworks-stand explosion. Her untimely funeral was being held that morning at 10:00 AM.

We had been waiting across the street until the last of the mourners departed the church. When my father shouted, "Ladders up!" we prepared to begin.

Our large commercial ladders were made of wood and could be adjusted to heights from sixteen to twenty-eight feet. Two ladders were placed against the church wall about eight feet apart. Next, Dad and his foreman, Duane, confidently scooted up separate ladders. At the top they each installed a metal ladder jack. These scaffolding devices attached to the top rung and a rung two steps lower, thus forming a triangular bracket securely hanging from the ladder. Then two eight-inch wide wooden planks, each twelve feet long, were carried up and placed between the two ladder jacks. Together they formed a perch that was sixteen inches wide and twelve feet long.

Standing on the ground, my neck wrenched as I looked upward, I watched as Dad and Duane worked in unison. At that young age I don't believe I fully understood the impact this "right of passage" was going to have on the rest of my life.

After a few minutes, my dad yelled, "Bring up a couple of roof jacks."

Yippie! I grabbed two jacks and peeled for the ladder. Roof jacks are similar to ladder jacks in that they form angles to create a level surface to stand on while working on steep slopes. In this case that level surface was only a single eight-inch wide wooden plank.

As I scaled the ladder I could use only one hand to grip the rungs because the other hand was holding the jacks. With each step up there was a moment when I had no hands holding onto the ladder. The higher I climbed, the more the ladder swayed, twisted and creaked.

When I was about twelve to fifteen feet up, the ladder developed a two-foot sway, back and forth. Well, maybe it was really more like one-foot of sway, but it felt like a lot. I thought to myself, while trying to act cool, *Am I going to die my first trip up the ladder?*

My visions of becoming the world's greatest roofer quickly turned to thoughts of falling to my death!

Approaching the top, I offered my payload to Dad's outreached hands. I think he was chuckling at the look of terror on my whiskerless young face. Without much hesitation, I began my descent back to the sanity of earth below.

Once down, I thought, *That wasn't too bad, I guess I can do it again.*

My next trip up was to carry roof shingles. Shingles are each approximately three feet long, one foot wide and about a quarter inch thick; each full bundle of roofing shingles weighs seventy-five to eighty pounds.

To begin, my dad suggested I only carry a third of a bundle under my arm. Real roofers carry a full bundle on their shoulder, one hand on the bundle to balance the load, while climbing up the ladder rungs with their free hand. This process is repeated many times per day per crewmember.

As I once again approached the top, things got more difficult. The ladder jacks were right above my head. To get the shingles up onto the planks above I had to grab the top ladder rung and lean way back while stepping up one more rung. Then, without dropping my load, I had to lift twenty-five to thirty pounds of roofing one-handed, up over my head, depositing them on the planks.

Once the shingles were up on the scaffolding I had to position them so they wouldn't fall off and hit me on the head while I was climbing back down.

After a few more trips up and down, the crew had advanced higher, to another scaffolding level. Then, after placing the shingles up on the overhead scaffolding, I too had to climb up onto the ladder scaffolding.

It's difficult to describe the fear that I had to overcome at that moment.

In order to get up onto that ladder scaffolding, I had to reach up and grab the metal ladder jack with one hand, the other hand clinching the planks. Then I had to step off the ladder, feet dangling out twenty feet in the air. By swinging my legs sideways I hooked my heel on the planks and twisted my body up onto the platform. From there I'm on my knees, trying to catch my balance.

Did I mention that we didn't use any safety ropes or railings?

Gaining my balance enough to stand up took a few seconds. The wind swirling around me was great for evaporating some the perspiration oozing out of my pores, but didn't seem to help at all with keeping my balance.

Ladder swaying, planks bowing and wind blowing, I felt like I was up there trying to balance on a beach ball.

Next I had to bend down and, using both hands, pick up the shingles and lift them up onto the roof jack. Roof jacks are only half as wide as the more spacious ladder jacks.

"Keep your balance or die!" was my new motto.

I remember looking up and seeing my dad casually working above me. I drew a deep breath, said a quick prayer and got back to work.

As I continued to climb up and down every few minutes, things started to get tough. The men had applied enough roofing to require a second level of roof scaffolding. That meant on my next trip up I had to climb one-handed up the ladder, crawl out onto the ladder scaffolding, then lift the shingles up onto the first level of roof scaffolding. After all that, in order to get the shingles up to where the other roofers were working, I had to somehow get up onto the first level of roof scaffolding too.

The reality of my making it to age fourteen faded away as I prepared myself for my next heart-pounding challenge. It was time to really test my nerves.

After placing the shingles up on the plank, I had to grab the corner of the roof jack—which was nailed in place with three small roofing nails—with one hand, then grab the plank with my other hand. As I lifted my feet off the safety of that perch I once again had to swing my legs high enough to catch my heel on the plank above. Twisting and pulling myself up onto the narrow plank took every ounce of strength and balance I possessed.

Did I mention the wind continued to blow, and still no safety railing surrounding my eight-inch wide job site? I felt like I was trying to work while balancing on a beach ball out on the ledge of a New York skyscraper.

As I stood on the plank with nothing but air around me, I had to bend down to pick up my cargo and lift those stupid shingles up onto the next plank. Thoughts like, *Why couldn't my dad own a shoe store?* raced through my terror-filled mind.

For some reason, the higher I got, the more difficult each task seemed. Occasionally, during a moment of confidence, I would watch the other roofers' constant efforts. These guys seemed as comfortable as though they were bowling. Watching them gave me the feeling that at least I had a chance of survival.

After relaxing there a bit, I realized my cozy thoughts were a little premature. Down-climbing this albatross was about all my frayed nerves could take. Most people never experience this kind of fear.

As I tried to climb down, I could not see the plank below. I lowered myself, wondering, *Did I miss that narrow plank? Do I need to go lower? Should I pull myself back up while I still have the strength?*

Finally, my tiptoes hit pay dirt. That wiggly old plank felt quite stable after having dangled in thin air three stories up.

Struggling to regain my composure, I realized I would have to make that onerous move many more times during the next few hours. Soon after six o'clock, my dad commanded the men to wrap up their work and call it a day.

I headed down and began cleaning up our mess on the ground. After six adrenalin-pumping hours, words can't describe the relief I felt as we rode home in the old roofing truck.

I believe my dad was pretty proud that I stuck it out like a real roofer. Hallelujah! I had just survived my first day on the job!

Robert Sherman was born in South Dakota to a hard working family during the summer of 1955. His sixth-grade teacher encouraged him to become a writer, but a heavy workload derailed that path. Not until well into his adult life was he able to begin his writing career with one book, *Quiet on the Set*, and five movie screenplays to his credit. He is still a roofer to this day.

Author Loren Flaugh today, with the original
New Holland baler from his story.

MAKING A LITTLE SPENDING MONEY

Loren Gaylord Flaugh

Like most teenage high school boys, making a little extra spending money was always a priority for me in the summertime. And it's a great way for someone young to start developing a good work ethic. A good work ethic can get someone far in life.

Being raised on a small family farm in Northwest Iowa, the various means of making some extra cash were never too difficult to come by. I walked many a soybean field seeking the volunteer corn, cockleburs and prickly thistle plants.

Farm life in the 1960s meant most farmers sowed a few acres of oats every spring, to be ready for harvest by mid-summer. Most farmers also had several acres of forage crops like alfalfa or clover, used in livestock feed rations.

When the rains were plentiful during the spring and summer growing season, forage crops might be mowed and baled as many as three, or even four times, until late September. The straw residue from the oat crop also needed to be raked and baled.

Because of the spring rains, the first hay cutting was almost always plentiful. The intoxicating aroma of newly mown hay wafting across the countryside was a pleasant fragrance that only lasted about a day.

Left lying out in the warm summer sun, the hay dries down, making the stems and leaves supple and suitable for storage.

29

After a day or two of drying down, the crop was raked into windrows for further drying, raked again to turn it over so the warm winds would dry it even more, so they could bale it a day or two later.

Not every farmer in the neighborhood owned their own baler. In our Baker Township neighborhood of O'Brien County, Vernon Kaiser was one nearby farmer who owned one. Vernon's baler of choice was the widely recognized bright red New Holland Super Hayliner 78, made in, where else, New Holland, Pennsylvania.

As a rule, many farmers mowed their hay crops at about the same time or within a few days of their neighbors. Vernon took his tractors, baler and hayracks on the road and moved throughout the neighborhood, baling one hayfield after the other. Baling everyone's crops took a week or two of his time for each cutting.

Vernon had a husky baling crew: Keith Iverson and me. We baled hay or straw in the hot summer sun and played baseball for the Paullina Panthers in the evenings. Iverson was a catcher and I played left field. Tossing heavy hay bales on the hayrack as high as ten feet sure helped build muscle. What a great work out!

But baling had its occupational safety hazards, too. Rolling across the hayfield, the hayrack seemed to find every deep badger hole or fox den in the field and lurched violently every time a wheel plunged into a seemingly bottomless hole.

Perhaps the greatest scourge was when the baler ingested a nest of nasty bumblebees. Out for vengeance, they'd swarm like a swirling storm around the machine or the hapless humans on the rack. Stinging the iron machine didn't work, but human flesh was easier to penetrate. At times, a frightened baler bailed off the rack to escape bees seeking retribution.

Another hazard was swinging the sharp bale hook at a bale and missing. I remember one incident when the sharp hook swung around after missing the end of the bale and impaled the forearm of the city kid stacking bales. A brief trip to the hospital for stitches closed the nasty puncture wound.

Lunchtime was often the best part of a hot afternoon. Sitting under the hayrack in the shade and being served lunch by the family whose hay was being baled was a great way to get rejuvenated. The food was often plentiful.

Standing on the hayrack and watching the mechanisms work was fascinating in its own way. The pick-up reel grabbed the windrow of hay and fed it into a chamber, where the hay was cut by a shiny sharp shear. A thick steel plate compressed each wad until enough stuff was there to make a seventy-pound bale.

Perhaps the most interesting inner workings to watch was how the twine was threaded around a bale, tied into a knot and cut. Little kids often struggle for weeks, months or years when first learning to tie a knot in their shoes. But somehow mankind figured out a way for a machine to tie a knot. The dexterity of the knotter was clearly the most specialized mechanism on the machine to watch.

A mechanical counter counted each bale that came shooting off the chute and into the waiting hands of the stacker. Stacking the perfect load was always a goal. Going around a corner on a steeply sloped side hill, only to have half the load tumble over onto the ground wasn't a pretty sight.

Two summers was the length of my tenure at stacking bales for Vernon Kaiser. I moved on through life; went to Vietnam in 1968; pursued a career in the petroleum industry; worked for an electrical engineering firm; then learned a little bit about writing when I wrote a weekly personal opinion column for a daily newspaper in El Dorado, Kansas in 1988. The *El Dorado Times* titled my columns, "The Mixed Bag."

Then, nearing forty-five years of age, my wife and I moved our family back home to Iowa. I continued writing, had some modest success getting published in magazines and newspapers, repaired farm machinery for six years and worked other odd jobs to make a living.

In the evenings, taking a stroll around Primghar was a great way to get some exercise. Walking twenty blocks or more in under a half hour wasn't too hard when I was fifty years old. Ten years later, I noticed it was taking longer to walk the same distance. But I guess that's a normal part of aging.

Often, my exercise route took me out past the O'Brien County Historical Museum, on past the golf course and a big loop around the south end of town.

One object on my route, located in an open-ended building at the historical museum, always left me wondering. The object seemed so familiar.

31

Parked along the north side of the building was an old, not so bright red anymore, New Holland Super Hayliner 78 baler.

Month after month, and year after year even, I silently wondered if this was indeed the same baler I had stood behind for two summers so long ago. Was it, after all these years, the same one?

Then, one day not too many years ago, curiosity finally got the better of me. I happened to meet up with Vernon Kaiser. After all these years, Vernon was still in good health, albeit fifty years older, just like his baler. I asked him, "What ever happened to that old New Holland baler you used to have?"

Kaiser answered, "I donated it to the O'Brien County Historical Museum many years ago."

A machine I came to know well in the summers of 1965 and '66 is within a short walking distance from where I live, and is likely to be around longer than I will.

Loren Flaugh lives in Primghar, Iowa, where he continues to enjoy writing feature stories on energy and renewable energy for *Wallaces Farmer* magazine. He's learned more about the high voltage electric grid in the past year than he would have ever imagined.

Photo provided by Diane Sue Fritz

CORN PICKER BEAUTY SHOP

Debi Marie Iske

Though I was born in Iowa and have lived most of my life here, for a few years my family farmed in south central Wisconsin.

My parents met and married in Iowa. My father farmed, and shortly after I was born, my parents heard of a farm to rent in Wisconsin. They moved there, with me and a few milk cows in tow. They rented a farm, which my dad worked with the livestock and a small piece of farmland on which he grew hay and corn to feed the animals. Our farm was beautiful, and they fell in love with the lush, rolling land.

A year after our move, my sister DeAnn was born. As we grew, DeAnn and I were always playing outside. Mom and Dad didn't worry at all about our making our way through the outbuildings and exploring the area, as long as our dog, Sporty, was with us. Sporty, a collie, kept a close eye on us.

One of our favorite places to go was behind one of the outbuildings, where an old, broken-down corn picker sat in a secluded spot, surrounded by weeds that included an endless growth of cockleburs. The corn picker was huge—at least it seemed huge to two little girls. Beneath it the space opened up to make a sheltered play area. DeAnn and I dragged all sorts of things to our "playhouse," and spent a good part of our days there when the weather permitted.

In the early 1970s, when I was about six years old, and DeAnn four, we decided we would play beauty shop.

From an early age I'd been fascinated by my mom's ritual with her hair. At night she would wash it, set the bangs and sides with Dippity-Do, then tape them down with the special pink tape bought for that purpose. Using more Dippity-Do, she'd roll up the rest of her hair in pink spongy rollers. I never tired of watching her, and it didn't take long before I was sure I'd make a pretty good hairdresser.

So it came about on one summer day that I decided I would perm my little sister's hair! DeAnn was all for it.

We searched around our play area for something that would work as perm rods. My eyes settled on the green spongy cockleburs that grew all around the corn picker. Perfect! The cockleburs certainly clung to Sporty's fur. They would work just as well, I reasoned, on human hair.

Together, DeAnn and I gathered a plentiful supply of the cockleburs until we were sure we had enough.

I'll never forget the sense of excitement I felt as I sat DeAnn down and got to work. She remained perfectly still as I separated her shoulder-length hair, only about a finger's width section at a time. Carefully I rolled the long strand around a cocklebur, all the way to her scalp.

The cocklebur held it firmly in place, just as I'd know it would.

Beauty is not a fast process. Young as we were, DeAnn and I already understood this. She never moved from her seat as I worked, meticulously rolling and rolling, strand after strand of her hair, up to the scalp.

When I was finally finished wrapping all of DeAnn's hair in the makeshift curlers, I stepped back to admire my handiwork. I was extremely proud of what I'd done. The weed-wrapped hair stood out from her scalp in a perfect sphere. It looked very much like, I realized, the Harlem Globetrotters we often watched on TV.

DeAnn and I crawled out of our play space. Eager to show Mom what I'd done, I took her by the hand and we ran to the house.

Mom must have seen us coming, because she had the back door open and was coming out before we even reached the first step.

"Look, Mom," I sang, "look what I did! She looks just like a Negro!"

There was an expression of horror on our mother's face.

Mom tried to get the cockleburs out of my sister's hair, but they held tight. She finally gave up, got the scissors and clipped DeAnn's hair nearly down to the scalp.

In my own defense, this was not the first time DeAnn had found herself with very little hair on her head. At east twice before, she had gotten hold of Dad's electric hair clippers and used them on herself. On those occasions Mom had to shave off nearly all of her hair just to repair the damage. DeAnn spent a good part of her pre-kindergarten years wearing caps and bonnets, but it wasn't *all* my doing.

This disaster didn't deter me from an interest in hair. By the time I was eight my dad had let me start cutting his hair. Before long I was also cutting Mom's and DeAnn's hair, and continued to do so until I graduated from high school and moved out.

I headed for Mason City, where I enrolled in cosmetology school. After getting my license, I worked as a hair stylist for many years.

I credit my little sister DeAnn with getting me started.

Debi Marie Iske lives in Everly, Iowa, where she still dabbles in hair cutting and styling for friends and family. She's married to Shaun, and has two sons, Cale and Skylar.

SLIDING INTO TURD BASE

Jolene Armsdale

Summer baseball games in our small town in Wisconsin were spontaneous affairs, and usually brought at least a dozen kids, all eager to play.

We didn't have fancy equipment. In fact, we had hardly any equipment at all. I had an old glove that had belonged to one of my brothers, and maybe that's why the boys let me play. Also, I was a tomboy and a pretty good ball player. As the only girl in my family, smack in the middle of seven kids, I got not only my brothers' hand-me-down sports equipment, but their clothes, as well. My mother had long ago given up on dressing me like a girl.

Other players brought whatever they could to the games. Bobby was a serious player, so he had a pretty decent bat, a Pee Wee Reese that he'd gotten for Christmas the year before.

Then there was Tank, a chubby kid who provided a baseball as well as the brown bag full of snacks his mother always sent with him, and TJ, who was just a lot of fun to have around.

As far as the bases, we improvised with whatever we could find lying around.

On this particular spring Saturday afternoon we had a larger than usual group of kids show up, and we scrambled to put our playing field together. "I got first base," Bobby yelled, trotting towards us with an old, dented blue and yellow metal California license plate in hand. Then Tank removed the lightweight sweatshirt he was wearing, folded it in a square and set it down in the dirt to act as second base. It was already pretty beat up, so he figured it was okay. Home base was a dirty flattened shirt box.

"We need one more," said Leo, who was in my grade at school but at least two years older because he'd been held back a bunch of times. Leo looked meaningfully at me.

For a minute I wondered what he was staring at, then realized he had his eye on the almost-new jacket from Woolworth's I was wearing, the one my brother Carl had given me and that he'd hardly worn at all.

"Oh, no, uh-uh," I said firmly, taking a step back.

"I got an idea," said TJ. He ran off across the field, to one of the pastures that flanked it. In that pasture were several brown and white cows. Before any of us knew what he was up to, TJ was climbing the fence. Then he was over it, stepping gingerly and looking down at the ground as he went. The cows stepped calmly aside. TJ bent down and poked a finger at the ground. When he turned and faced us, he held something high in the air. "Got it!" he shouted.

We couldn't believe it. TJ was holding a large, semi-dry cow patty. "Turd base," he crowed as he came back over the fence.

We chose teams. I was on the same team as Bobby, TJ and Tank, the opposite team as Leo, which was okay with me as he kept mumbling under his breath about ". . . letting a girl play."

We found our places and began a rousing game. Our team won the coin toss, so we were first up to bat. We'd just gotten started when a couple of girls from our school arrived to watch. Shirley and Sandra sat on a grassy patch at the edge of our playing field. They had their border collie, Bruce, with them. Even though school was out, the sisters both wore skirts, which they arranged neatly around them. Bruce settled in beside them.

Bobby went to bat first, and he bent dramatically at the waist, swinging his Pee Wee Reese in a horizontal arc and glaring at Leo, who was pitching for the other side.

Bobby hit the ball—hard. The *CRACK* sounded like a gunshot. He dropped the bat and ran with all he had, his legs pumping like he was in a marathon. He'd passed first base, the California license plate, and was headed for second base when Bruce, excited by this sudden activity, as well as the many kids were who shouting at Bobby to "Go! Go!" decided to join the game. The dog jumped up and raced out into the field. Shirley and Sandra got to their feet and yelled for him to come back.

Bruce reached second base before Bobby did. He grabbed the folded-up sweatshirt in his teeth and took off with it.

"Hey!" Bobby yelled. He veered off course to chase after the dog. A couple of other kids joined in the pursuit, which Bruce seemed to see as a terrific new game.

In the meantime, a player named Henry picked up the ball and threw it to where second base was supposed to be. The player there caught it, stomped his foot in the dirt and said, "Ye'r out!"

Bobby stopped chasing Bruce to address this insult. "It was interference," he said.

There was much arguing for the next several minutes, with both teams going toe-to-toe, defending their positions. Bruce, now that he wasn't being chased, sat down and dropped the sweatshirt.

Finally it was decided that Bobby would have made it to second base without the interference, so that's where he went.

Next it was my turn at bat. I picked up the Pee Wee Reese from the ground and lifted it to my shoulder.

Leo returned to his spot as pitcher. "I'll toss it nice and easy for you," he said to me.

"Don't do me any favors."

And right at that moment, from a block and a half away, we all heard it: "Jolene! Joleeeeene! Time to come home!"

I froze, horrified. It was my mother's voice.

"Joleeeeene. Joleeeeene!" a few of the players from the other team mocked.

Leo grinned and straightened, letting the hand that held the ball drop to his side. "Better go home, Jolene. Your mommy's calling you."

I jutted out my chin. "I'm waiting," I told Leo.

He threw the pitch.

I swung and—hit! The ball arced high in the air, so that three players all ran for it at the same time, looking up into the late afternoon sky as gravity took over and it plummeted back to earth. I was already running. My feet barely touched the ground as I rounded first base.

"Run, Jo, run!" shouted Shirley and Sandra. My team was also yelling for me to keep going, so I did. Past second base, headed for third.

I had to rely on my teammates to let me know what was happening in the outfield, so when I heard them cry, "They got it, Jo! Slide! *Sliiiiiiide!*"

I slid. But not feet-first. Instead I hit the ground face first, arms outstretched in front of me. At the last second before my body made contact with the dirt I remembered that I was still wearing the jacket I had earlier refused to relinquish. In the next second I remembered exactly *what* third base was made of.

Too late. Momentum was carrying me forward. The cow patty, which had looked reasonably firm when TJ had brought it from the pasture, loomed in my line of vision, and as I hit it I knew it was not nearly as firm as we'd thought.

Instinct drove me to shut my eyes and mouth, but cow dung went up my nose, into my hair and down the front of my shirt.

The cries of "Slide Jo!" stopped immediately. As I sat up in the dirt, the silence around me was complete—until it was broken by Leo, who began laughing his big booming laugh that got a few others chuckling. I heard Shirley and Sandra's cries of sympathy, accompanied by "Eeeww!"

Tank ran over to where I was sitting, took my hand and pulled me to my feet.

In the distance, I heard, "Joleeeeen, time to come home!" Mom didn't yet sound impatient. Had it really only been a few seconds since my mother had started calling my name?

"Here, Jo," Tank said, handing me the clean washcloth his mother always included in his brown paper bag of snacks.

"Thanks." I used the washcloth to wipe off some of the mess from my hands and arms, but even I knew there was no saving this situation. My mother's voice began to take on a tone that I recognized. "I better go. I'll get this back to you," I told Tank.

He lifted his hand in a sort of "don't bother" gesture.

Leo was still laughing, but as I walked away from the field and in the direction of home, they quickly forgot about me and I heard their voices as they got the game going again.

My mother took the sight of me with a characteristic lack of surprise. She helped me wash the dung out of my hair, and as I explained to her how I'd come to be in such a state, I thought I saw her trying to suppress a smile.

Yes, I had to tell her that I'd slid into turd base.

Jolene Armsdale grew up in a small town in central Wisconsin, living there until she left for college in 1960, after which she worked as a nurse in Eau Claire and married her childhood sweetheart. Ten years ago she and her husband, Theodore, known to his friends as "Tank," retired to Arizona.

Photo provided by Jolene Armsdale

SOCIAL DANCING CLASS

David Peterson

One of the first things I learned when I arrived on campus as a college freshman was that all of us freshmen were required to wear beanies for the first three weeks of classes. I presume the reason was so the upperclassmen would know precisely who to pick on, as though they couldn't have figured it out on their own.

I had studied the college course catalog and had selected courses that I wanted to take the first term. My planning went out the window when they herded us freshmen into a gymnasium filled with faculty members sitting behind tables to help us register. The professor I was assigned to was a wild-eyed guy with curly hair and thick glasses who I immediately nicknamed McGoo, in my mind.

Without asking me what I planned to major in or what courses I wanted to take, McGoo filled in five courses on my registration form. He said I needed one more credit – maybe a physical education course would do. That was fine with me, since I had played high school sports and the thought of taking a course in football or tennis appealed to me.

"Here's one that will fit your schedule," McGoo said, and he registered me for Social Dancing. And then he sent me on my way before I could mutter an objection.

"Social Dancing?" I thought. What kind of a phy. ed. course was that?

After a little contemplation, I finally convinced myself McGoo may have done me a favor by signing me up for Social Dancing. You see, I was considered to be quite the dancer in high school.

On the first day of class, it appeared that most of the guys, except for three of us green freshmen wearing beanies, knew each other. They were big guys, muscular, loud, and rowdy. Obviously they were upper classmen and knew the ropes.

It was also apparent from listening to their conversation that they were all on the football team. Even though I was just a green freshman, I was smart enough to know that any class attracting so many football players had to be a cushy course. Show up for class, put in your time, look interested, and you could count on an "A." Maybe McGoo wasn't such a bad guy after all.

The class met in a practice gymnasium with a regulation size basketball court but no seating other than several benches on either side of the court. We guys sat on one side of the court and the girls sat on the other side. I sized up the girls and counted them—eleven in all. About half of them were wearing beanies and looked as clueless as I did. They were a typical cross section of the girls I had observed on campus—tall ones, short ones, skinny ones, chubby ones, pretty ones, homely ones, and some who fell in between.

The teacher, Miss Roberts, closed the door about five minutes after the hour, allowing plenty of time for the stragglers to find the room before she started class. She walked to the center of the auditorium, halfway between the benches and called the class roll. Every person on her list was present.

"Sometimes there is a little confusion about what Social Dancing class amounts to, so let me explain," she started. "In this class, I will teach you common ballroom dance styles such as the tango, mambo, waltz, polka, fox trot, and others so you will be more socially graceful and confident with your dancing, and in other social situations, throughout your entire adult life."

Uh, oh. I was a rock 'n' roll dancer and could be in trouble here.

Next, Miss Roberts carefully counted the number of males and females. I counted along as she pointed to each of us—eleven females and twenty-one males. She frowned a little bit at the imbalance.

"Well," she said, "since this class largely consists of dancing with a partner, and since we have an uneven number of men and women, at times it appears that two males will have to dance together on occasion."

All of us guys groaned. All of the gals laughed. Damn that McGoo.

"The first dance we will learn is the waltz. It is one of the simplest dance steps, yet one of the most commonly used. If you are a good waltzer, you can fit into almost any social dancing situation. Watch my feet and listen as I describe the steps—the very simple steps—used in the waltz."

Miss Roberts glided across the floor by herself, demonstrating the steps in the waltz as she called out the steps to match her footwork—"*Step*-step, step; *step*-step, step; *step*-step, step; *step*-step, step."

Next, Miss Roberts recruited one of the guys to help her demonstrate how the waltz was danced by a couple. Since he wasn't wearing a beanie, apparently he was an upperclassman who had taken a class or two from Miss Roberts previously.

Miss Roberts showed how the man and woman should position their hands and then they were off, gliding gracefully across the floor as Miss Roberts called out, "*Step*-step, step; *step*-step, step; *step*-step, step."

"Now it's your turn," Miss Roberts said. "Grab a partner."

There was a mad scramble by us twenty-one guys trying to grab one of the eleven women. When the dust settled, eleven lucky guys had paired up with the eleven women, which left ten of us, including the three of us wearing beanies, standing there trying not to look at each other. Double-damn that McGoo.

"Go ahead, you guys, pair up—and decide which one of you will be the man and which will be the woman," Miss Roberts said with a little smile.

The rest of the class, especially the lucky eleven guys who'd gotten women for partners, howled with delight.

"But, we will change partners," Miss Roberts continued, "so all of you guys will get your chance to dance with the women."

A huge guy, maybe six-foot-five and three hundred pounds, tapped me on the top of my beanie and said, "May I have this dance, my dear?"

And that's how I ended up dancing with the captain of the football team. Thanks, McGoo. Thanks a lot.

David Peterson was raised on a farm in southern Minnesota and attended what is now called Minnesota State University. He taught four years in a high school and thirty-four years in a community college and is the author of twenty-four books. His newest book, *Memoirs of a Recovering Teacher*, will be published in May 2013.

OLDER BROTHER AND ARTHUR MURRAY TEACH DANCING IN A HURRY

Linda J. Ireland

Growing up in Iowa, I knew that someday I'd become a dancer. I dreamt of New York stages and Hollywood film sets—completely ignorant of the outside world where pudgy little girls with fat knees do not one day beautiful ballerinas make. I believed I could do anything.

That was my mother's fault. She was a feminist before the word ever seeped through the airwaves. She wouldn't have cared what her philosophy was called, anyway, since she never put much stock in other people's opinions. She believed people rarely know what they're talking about.

She may have been right, since she herself told me unrealistic things like: "You can do or be anything you want. All you have to do is dream it." What kind of advice is that for a young girl in Iowa? But I believed it, and it led me into all sorts of scrapes.

Like the night my twenty-one year-old, six-foot, hairy biker brother told me I'd never be a dancer because I wasn't graceful.

As he towered over my four-foot, fourth-grade, stocky frame in our living room, I couldn't see his face. He was backlit by yellowed light streaming from the kitchen through the shelves holding metal, soapstone, and wooden elephants my father brought from India after World War II.

Glaring at the spot where his face should have been above his black-leather-clad torso, I watched the elephants marching into his right ear and out his left as he presented me with a challenge: "I'll prove you're not graceful. Try kicking your leg over my head."

So I did. First I dreamt we were in Africa and he was in danger from a herd of wild elephants, and then I imagined I'd spent the previous year in China studying martial arts with a master. I pictured my leg rising toward his right ear, taking out the elephants going into his brain, and then swinging over his head and destroying the rest of the elephants on the way down.

Physics and gravity foiled me. As one foot neared the top of his head, my other foot came out from under me. The thud of my body hitting the floor shook the house.

I woke to find myself staring up to see my fearless mother scolding a towering, laughing Heathen without a Lick of Sense about his Endless Tricks and Antics.

That night my brother nicknamed me Grace, to indicate what I lacked. I ignored the nickname and, following Mom's you-can-be-anything-you-dream motto, dreamt that my brother was a gnat on the wall I could shoo away with a flick of my hand.

And I spent long hours in my room, spinning Elvis records on the turntable, and twirling and dipping in front of the mirror.

In junior high, I made friends with a neighbor who shared my dream of dancing. Apparently our town was rife with early feminists; her mom had told her the same thing my mom told me, that she could be anything she wanted. Melanie was leaning toward being a juvenile delinquent, since she liked free cigarettes from cute boys and free clothes from J.C. Penney's. I tried to keep her focused on the dream we shared.

It was 1967, and go-go girls were everywhere: shindigging across America on stages and in cages, ponying their feet and swimming their arms through the air, jerking and monkeying and shimmying with dress fringes vibrating like miniature willow branches in a hot summer wind. Melanie and I thought there could be no better life, so we got busy practicing for it.

Her mother's sofa made the perfect stage. A '50s-style boxy structure with flat, wide arms covered with nubby fabric and no padding, it gave us plenty of room to prance even with our go-go boots on. We enlisted Melanie's younger brothers and sisters as our audience, although we had to front them admission money and they weren't very good about repaying it. Whenever Melanie's mom left the living room, we'd round up the kids, arrange the pole lamp as spotlights, and shimmy and shake our hearts out. We knew it was only a matter of time before a talent scout discovered us.

But eventually Melanie opted for the life of a runaway and ended up in Mitchellville—that infamous girls' house of detention adults had hung over my head all my life. The standard warning, "Don't do that again unless you want to end up in Mitchellville," was used for every transgression from dancing on sofa arms to stealing clothes to running away with cute boys who smoked. In a world where you can become anything, all things become sort of equal.

So once again I was alone with my dancing dreams—and my big brother. At least he had stopped calling me Grace. Since I'd had whooping cough that, according to him, made me croak like a big old rowdy bullfrog, he had started calling me Toad.

My brother had a Harley on which to go roaring out into the world, so he learned about kinds of dancing I'd never seen. One day he told me if I wanted to prepare for the kind of dancing career I was likely to have, I should wear my nightgown and practice dancing around a pole in the basement. But when Mom caught me, she informed me that some things I might dream about I would never become—because she wouldn't let me.

Then she clomped up the stairs, muttering that she was going to find that brother of mine and give him a serious talking to about the kind of influence he was having on me.

Having discovered I could have only dreams that weren't too exotic, I set aside my dancing aspirations for most of my high school years and focused on practical things, such as home economics lessons on sewing aprons and cooking hot dogs in crescent rolls.

I still danced to Elvis music in my room, but since I'd finally figured out that chunky girls rarely made it to stage or screen, I had decided to become an Elvis impersonator. I worked up a really nice hip-shaking, knee-swerving, shoulder-twisting, lip-curling routine to "You Ain't Nothin' but a Hound Dog."

And once again my brother dashed my dreams. I had gathered the family together to watch the show I was planning to take to Vegas. My brother shouldn't even have been there, since he refused to pay the admission price, but after we scuffled for a while, Mom said if we didn't just shut-up and get on with it, there would be no show. So I let him stay.

Though I performed superbly, my brother said I looked just like his old hound dog scrambling up the muddy bank of Black Hawk Creek with a five-pound catfish flapping in his droopy jaws.

Then, years later, I saw an ad for a position at Arthur Murray's Dance Studio. I thought my dancing dreams had disappeared, but it turned out they were merely in remission. I answered the ad with trepidation, thinking my weight might be a barrier, even with all my previous experience of dancing on sofa arms and around basement poles. But they hired me, and during my six weeks of unpaid training I added the fox trot, waltz, cha-cha, tango, mambo, and rhumba to my already fairly impressive repertoire.

Arthur Murray's required me to wear four-inch heels all day and still smile. At night I collapsed into bed with moans and groans, and in the morning crawled to the bathroom and soaked my swollen, bleeding feet in warm water until I could walk. But I didn't care. I was dancing!

The job also meant travel. On a riverboat in Minneapolis, I sipped champagne from a caviar-lined fountain between waltzes. In Chicago I slept in a room at the Playboy Club and fox-trotted across the Aragon Ballroom. I didn't care that I had to sew my own ball gowns and pay for hotel rooms and food. I was a dancer!

Then suddenly my career ended, and of course my brother played a role in it.

After I had mastered lessons in fancy footwork, the dance studio started teaching me sales techniques. I was instructed to dance close to the students and make them feel sexy. I was told to convince them that taking out a second mortgage for exorbitantly expensive lessons would bring them love, sex, and happiness. I was directed to rub up against them if necessary, to close the deal.

This was a whole new kind of dancing for me. I pictured my students. They were nice people. Most were not young; many were lonely. None were wealthy. I knew I couldn't treat them that way, but I didn't want to quit because I loved the dancing, teaching, and traveling.

Finally, I turned to my brother for help. He refused to discuss anything until we were on his Harley, so I agreed to a ride.

With sand in my eyes and bugs in my nose, between demands that he slow down to eighty so I would live to see thirty, I screamed my dilemma into his ear.

He thought about it for a few miles, then cocked his head and howled: "Toad, it's okay to be ornery with people you love—that's just teasing. But to fool people into thinking they'll find love where they won't—why, that's just plain mean. That you don't wanna do."

The next day I quit my job at Arthur Murray's, and danced away from there in a hurry.

Linda Ireland is a freelance writer, editor, and artist who lives and works in the Waterloo/Cedar Falls, Iowa, area. She edits books and other publications, writes, teaches drawing and painting classes, and enjoys scrapbooking and gardening. This story is dedicated to the memory of her brother, Edwin Paul Ireland, who was not only a brother to Linda, but also a father, a teacher, and a friend.

THE YELLOW MONSTER

Marie Wells

During the Great Depression in the early nineteen thirties, my family moved to a rundown farm west of Milford, Iowa. Dad was an excellent farmer, but he struggled trying to make a living on it.

After school each day, my three older brothers, Dale, Glen and Orville, and I had many outdoor chores to do. The older two boys carried heavy pails of grain to all of the animals and cleaned the horse and cow stalls. Orville and I gathered eggs from the hen house and grove and picked up bushel baskets of smelly corncobs from the hog pen to feed the voracious appetite of the ancient cookstove. It gobbled the corncobs up continuously when heating water and cooking food for the family.

Before heading out to do chores, the four of us usually had a home-baked cookie and a glass of milk while listening to our favorite radio program, "Jack Armstrong, the All-American Boy." What wonderful adventures Jack and his uncle had! I wished we could have a real adventure, but with all of the hard work to do on the farm, there was little time for adventures.

During the week Mother and Dad worked from dawn until dark, but Dad believed Sunday should be a day of rest for man and beast. Apparently that didn't apply to woman, since Mother always stayed home from church to prepare a delicious Sunday dinner for her family of eight.

Sister Mildred, Dad and I attended church and Sunday school in the one-room Center School, which also served as a church. On Sunday afternoons Dad liked to go for a drive to see how well the neighbors' crops were growing compared to his. Most of us liked to go along with him.

One Sunday afternoon in May, Dad drove along the dirt road a mile south of our home. About a half-mile down that road, we saw a huge yellow digging machine in a field near the fence. Dad drove by it slowly.

"Dad," I called from the back seat, "can we stop and look at that big machine?"

"Not this time," said Dad as he kept on checking out the neighbors' crops.

The next Saturday morning, when Orville and I were outdoors playing with our homemade clay marbles, I said, "I wish we could see that big yellow machine again. It was a monster."

Orville thought for a moment. "Maybe we can," he said excitedly.

Like true conspirators, we plotted and planned how we would manage to get another look at it. This could be a real adventure, I thought, and shivered with anticipation. Of course we didn't tell anyone about our plans. We knew if we told, our family would never let us go.

After lunch that sunny day, Orville and I ran out to the big red barn. The family thought we were going to play with the kittens, as we often did. Instead, we ran through the barn, out the far door and into the barnyard. Down the cow path between fenced-in fields, and into the pasture we raced. Across the pasture we flitted like two bright butterflies that had scented some fragrant red clover.

"There it is," Orville shouted. "There's the Yellow Monster."

"The Yellow Monster," I echoed, hardly able to believe we were so close to it.

Over the fences we clambered and into the field where the Yellow Monster lived. For a glorious hour we admired it, climbed on and over its yellow body, sat on its throne-like seat and stood up inside its massive wheels.

Then thunder crashed around us, lightning flashed and huge cold raindrops splattered down upon our bare heads. We scrambled down, raced over the fences and fled through the pasture toward our own warm homestead as the rain began to fall.

Halfway home we heard the rattling of our old Dodge car. Over the nearest hill it rumbled, our determined-looking Dad at the wheel and our worried-faced Mother beside him. Dad stopped the car, leaped out and grabbed the two of us.

He soundly whomped each of our bottoms and thrust us into the back seat. While we were riding home through the pounding rainstorm, Mother explained that the entire family had been searching for us for over an hour. When they thought we might have gone into the pasture, they'd the terrible fear that the cow with the new baby calf might have attacked us.

We whimpered in the back seat, truly sorry we had worried our parents and siblings.

The next day, however, Orville and I both agreed that the great adventure we'd had with the Yellow Monster had been well worth the price we'd paid!

Marie Wells is a retired elementary teacher. She likes to read, write, and tutor, play cards and take part in church activities. Marie lives in a one hundred twenty year old home with her sixteen-pound cat, Peanut.

Photo provided by Gary Arp

SOWING WILD OATS ON WHEELS

Rev. Gary Arp

It seems all of my wild oats sowing involved a set of wheels! I was born in 1934, son of Adolph and Betty Kolls Arp. From the time I was about four years old until I graduated from high school and moved away from home, our family lived on a farm, first in northwest Iowa a few miles south of Lake Park and then southwest Minnesota a few miles north of Lake Park. My great grandparents had left Germany to settle in Scott County Iowa, and later moved to Jackson County, Minnesota.

My first set of wheels was a scooter. I'm told that even at an early age I managed to get into trouble.

When I was seven years old, I begged my dad to buy me pony. A pony consumes feed meant for livestock, so Dad bought a bicycle for me instead. It was a new Schwinn, top of the line. I wasn't real happy about it, but at least I could make it go fast. The trouble was, I couldn't ride well enough to make it go in a straight line.

One day, going full tilt, I ran right into the outhouse! The collision sprung the fork on the bike so the front wheel was smashed against the frame. That pretty much ended my time with that set of wheels.

When I was old enough to get my driver's license we were already living in Minnesota. Dad would never let me drive the family car, but he let me drive our old 1940 Chevy pickup with the wooden box.

I was not happy having to drive a pickup truck. What self-respecting girl wanted to ride in a pickup?

But one night Dad agreed to let me take the truck to a school activity. The Sioux Valley school was two and a half miles east of our farm, and I was given strict orders to drive directly to school and back—no joy riding!

One mile north of the school was the famous (or infamous) Sioux Valley Log Cabin dance hall. I told my best friend, Ronnie Fick, I would take him home after the event, even though it was not exactly on my way home.

On the way to his place we decided to swing by the Log Cabin, just to see who was there. We wouldn't even stop, we vowed. And it was sort of on the way to Ronnie's house.

As we neared his place, suddenly we found the pickup coasting to a stop. An axle had broken. This was not good!

I tried to think of how we might get that thing back on the road to my home, but it was no use. The axle had slipped out, the tire was against the box and the truck absolutely couldn't be moved.

Ronnie's dad had to give me a ride home. I was prepared for the worst, but I guess Dad decided I had suffered so much worrying about what he was going to do to me that he just asked, "Did you learn anything from this?"

I assured him I had.

My only first cousin, Sheryl Arp, and her mother had moved to Reno, Nevada, when we were both about four years old. I didn't see Sheryl again until she came to visit us in Minnesota. Dad decided to let me use the car, a 1947 Chevy Fleetline Aerosedan, to take Sheryl roller-skating in Arnolds Park.

One of my buddies was there. He drove a 1941 Chevy, and we decided it would be a good idea to race back to Lake Park on Highway 9.

I was ahead, with the pedal to the metal, doing about eighty-five miles an hour. Looking in the rear view mirror, I saw a pair of headlights behind my buddy's car, coming up on us fast. I suspected it was a cop, but the speed limit at that time was "safe and reasonable" and I figured eighty-five was both safe and reasonable so I kept the foot feed to the floor.

But when the car sped past us I saw it was a 1947 Ford, and within a mile I could no longer even see its taillights. I said to my cousin, "Man I gotta have me one of those!"

After graduating from high school I went to work for Arco Dehydrating Company in Lake Park. The first summer I drove truck, and the second summer I worked wherever I was needed, either driving a truck or running the chopper.

The plant ran twenty-four hours a day and we worked twelve-hour shifts.

One night, when I was running the chopper, there were a few minutes of time between trucks to pick up the chopped hay. We were chopping alfalfa on a farm owned by a man who was rumored to be about "a half bubble off level." The story was that he hoarded things in his barn and might shoot anyone who got too close. Who knows whether any of it was true?

When the next truck arrived in the field the driver jumped out, yelling, "Frankie just jumped on George's truck!" Frankie was a local kid who loved to play tricks on people.

Oh boy, this was not good. George was a skittish guy, and it was hard telling what Frankie might do. He could end up getting them both killed.

I jumped behind the wheel of the truck that had arrived and we took off after them. But it was no use. We couldn't catch them.

We found out later that Frankie had jumped from the truck box onto the roof of the cab, which would be enough to scare anyone half to death. He then began dropping chopped hay on the windshield in front of the driver. George turned on the windshield wipers. Frankie reached down and grabbed a wiper.

George slammed on the brakes.

Fortunately Frankie had his leg hooked between the cab and the box, so he didn't fly off, but he fell forward so he was hanging upside down, staring straight into George's frightened face!

The crew at the plant said George came flying into the yard and jumped out of the truck, yelling, "He's after me! He's after me!"

When I had enough money for a down payment on a car, I found a used black 1949 Ford V8 with an overdrive transmission. It was my pride and joy. It would do ninety miles an hour in second overdrive, and in high gear it would put the speedometer past a hundred! There weren't many guys who had a car that could beat me in a race. The Olds Rocket 88 was about the only one I couldn't handle.

In my '49 Ford I went courting my girlfriend and future bride, Marjorie Davis. After we were married it took us to Wichita, Kansas, where I went to work for Boeing. In 1958 I traded it for a new one—a Ford, of course—which I tried out on the new Kansas Turnpike.

While working for Boeing I also attended Wichita University, and in 1961 I entered Concordia Theological Seminary in Springfield, Illinois.

One of my classmates had been a racecar driver in his former life. The local racetrack featured a race for "clunkers." My buddy talked me into buying an old junked Cadillac and entering it in the clunker race. During my first race I got hit by another car and slammed into a wall. That ended my racing career!

The oats I sow now are not quite so wild, but when I can do it legally I still enjoy driving fast—220 kilometers per hour (135 MPH) on the German Autobahn, with Marjorie saying, "That's enough, Gary, that's enough! That's enough, Gary, that's enough!"

And, whether I'm driving my V10 F250 pickup or my 2.0 Turbo VW Passat, I still can't resist being the first one off the line when the light turns green.

Rev. Dr. Gary Arp is a minister in the Lutheran Church Missouri Synod (LCMS). He is now retired and serves as part-time chaplain for IDE at the University of Iowa Hospitals and still conducts services for pastors who need someone to fill in. He and his wife, Marjorie, live in Marion, Iowa.

A WAGON FULL OF PRAIRIE GOLD

Marilyn Kratz

Growing up on a farm, my siblings and I usually had enough to do to keep from being bored. We had the whole farmyard and its surrounding shelterbelt of thickly growing elms in which to roam and play pretend games. Dogs, cats, an occasional half-grown tamed rooster, bucket calves, or runt pigs to raise kept us entertained when we weren't busy with chores.

But sometimes we wanted something new to do. And that's when we asked Mama to let us walk the half-mile to our Aunt Viola and Uncle Art's farm. Viola was my mom's sister, married to Art, who was my dad's brother. They had no children of their own, and being doubly related and living so close, they seemed almost like another set of parents to us.

We'd pull our rusty old red wagon along, filling it with the prairie gold of dandelions on the way to Art and Viola's farm. The hot summer sun shone down, making the warm earth, ripening grasses, and pungent weeds release their unique aromas. Wild roses on the far side of the ditch beckoned us with blossoms that always appeared much brighter pink than those within reach beside the graveled road. Bees droned their happy hum, punctuated by the sharp clear call of meadowlarks sitting on fence posts.

The rattle of our dandelion-filled wagon and our shouts of "Come see what we brought you, Viola!" as we ran into her yard, sent her skittish flock of white chickens squawking and flapping away.

Viola would open the screen door on their small house and welcome us with a big smile and her booming voice. Then she'd serve us lemonade and store-bought cookies, a real treat for us since we had only home-baked cookies at our house.

I still recall some of her favorite expressions. She'd always say "whatcha-ma-call-it" when she couldn't think of the name of something. If you asked how she was, she'd say, "Fine as frog's hair." And if she were upset about something, she'd boom out a "Hey!" that made you hope it wasn't directed at you.

I can still picture her in a flowered cotton housedress, her black hair held in place with a thin hairnet. She was plump, just like my mom. The plain furnishings in her home reflected her no-nonsense demeanor, which may have turned some people away but we loved her just the way she was.

After our treat, we'd beg to see her glow-in-the-dark ring, which she kept in a tray in her bedroom. She'd let us take it into the closet to see it glow. How I wish I had that ring now. It would be the perfect remembrance of that special lady.

When we'd exhausted all the entertainment possibilities inside the house, we'd ask our aunt, "Where's Art?" We knew our wiry uncle was always ready for some roughhousing. His blue eyes never failed to twinkle when he saw us.

I remember one summer day when our uncle, wearing his usual striped denim overalls and blue chambray shirt, was building a high new fence attached to the back of his barn. He had just pounded in the last staple holding the barbed wire onto strong wooden posts when we came running out of the house. Inside the pen, about a dozen yearling shorthorn calves, which Art would fatten for market, milled about.

"Hi, Art!" we shouted, arms waving as we ran to the barn, wagon rattling along behind us. "Whatcha doing?"

The calves, not used to the noise and actions of four children, bolted, broke down the new fence and ran off to the far corner of the pasture.

At first our uncle just stood there with his mouth open. But when he looked at us and saw the terror on our faces, all he could do was laugh.

"You nincompoops!" he yelled, and hearing him call us by his favorite nickname, we knew we were forgiven.

I don't remember what my parents said when they heard about the damage we had caused, which my dad likely ended up helping to repair. I don't believe we were even punished for it.

But I do remember the love we felt that summer afternoon when we brought our beloved aunt and uncle a wagon full of prairie gold.

Marilyn Kratz is a freelance writer from Yankton, South Dakota. She has had four books and nearly 600 magazine stories, articles, and poems published. She writes a nostalgia column for a Yankton weekly, and is a regular contributor to *Living Here*, a regional magazine published in Yankton. She is a retired elementary teacher.

STRAW AND HAY

Debra Dunn Kaczmarek

My only entanglement with pop music was a brief infatuation with Herman's Hermits and their unforgettable tune, "I'm Henry the Eighth, I Am." For several weeks, it must have been, I shelved my beat-up Columbia Masterworks LP of "Messiah—Christmas Music" to duet—oh, maybe three million times, always at maximum volume—with Peter Noone, the group's lead singer.

This was a remarkable departure from my devotion to classical music. I surmise that I made an exception for "Henry the Eighth" because it had clear literary and historical connections and so didn't do violence to my self-image as a budding intellectual. Whatever my rationale, it didn't fly with Dad—at least not after the three millionth run-through.

One early evening, Dad rose without warning from his customary seat at the kitchen table and careened into the living room, where we had the phonograph set up and where I was lying flat on my back, letting rip with the Hermits, albeit a few octaves higher.

I don't remember Dad saying a word. But he bent over, grasped the 45 in his massive left hand, while balancing his whisky-and-sugar-water cocktail in his right, and crumbled the disc into shiny black shards.

I took it hard. The dashing of another dream. Fortunately, a few weeks later Mr. Riemersma, our high school choir director, assigned me a Mozart aria ("Voi, che sapete") for the upcoming solo and ensemble contest. Opining that I had a voice meant for opera he advised me to scrupulously avoid acquiring deadly "pop" techniques.

Whew! What a close call! Dad's apparent orneriness had actually been part of God's plan to reveal my true destiny. Herman and those Hermits of his would have to make it the rest of the way without me. I was heading for La Scala!

But first I had to survive high school, something I could not have done without strategically-positioned piles of straw and hay. Let me explain.

Dunn family lore is peppered with unkind references to my driving abilities, which admittedly were not at first all they might have been. Some of my failings in this area had to do with plain old lack of skill. It's tricky to drive on loose gravel. Ask anybody.

Other failings had to do with plain old lack of common sense, as driving while reading Mom's letters from crazy Uncle Ray was behavior unworthy of a member of the Clay Central Honor Roll. But most of the time, my driving *faux pas* were directly traceable to the sub-standard vehicles Dad provided for my use.

There were many such vehicles, wrecks Dad had picked up somewhere for a song and then breathed new, albeit brief, life into. But one car in particular sticks in my memory—the one without brakes. No, I don't mean tricky brakes or squeaky brakes. I don't mean brakes that pulled or grabbed. I mean NO BRAKES. Emergency or otherwise. I don't remember make, model, or color—only its brakelessness.

By the time I took to piloting that particular car, I had a full year of licensed driving under my belt. I was a very busy high school senior with lots of after-school activities and twice-weekly early morning appointments with the pastor of St. Louis Catholic Church in Royal.

Late in my junior year, I'd decided to become a Catholic, and Fr. Robert Kirschbaum was instructing me on Tuesday and Thursday mornings, before classes began at the high school. Dad had no interest in encouraging either my extracurricular involvement or my religious conversion. When he was well into his cups, Dad often claimed to be of the enlightened opinion that parents shouldn't interfere with their children's religious choices. Kids should be free to make their own decisions about religion, he said—but, for the love of God, he hadn't meant we could choose *that* religion!

Now that I think about it, I wonder if Dad had assumed a brakeless vehicle would put the brakes on some of the activities that kept me away from the milk barn, where, in his opinion, I belonged. Then again, maybe he just had lots of confidence in me.

These days, not many parents allow their teenagers to drive vehicles without brakes. Even in the 1960s, it wasn't common. But it wasn't as dangerous as it sounds.

First of all, once I got the car up Schutknechts' hill, a maneuver that required steady acceleration, I passed into land as flat as a bowling alley. Heck, it was so flat that on a clear day we could almost make out the Royal water tower a full six miles away.

Seeing an approaching vehicle a mile or more off wasn't any kind of challenge, especially if we were in the middle of a dry spell, when a fast-moving pick-up would send up a cloud of black dust to rival the one that carried Dorothy to Oz. So, really, driving without brakes was mostly about timing. If I saw a vehicle in the distance, I adjusted my speed so as not to meet said vehicle at the next intersection. Not a problem.

Things got a little tricky about a mile outside Royal, where the road curved sharply just past Coach McDonnell's hobby farm. It was important to begin cutting back on the gas at least a quarter mile before the curve, just as I passed the Koenig place. Otherwise, centrifugal force would kick in, overwhelming the front passenger door latch and sending my carefully completed homework sliding across the bench seat and off into the ditch. On Mondays, Wednesdays, and Fridays, when one of my siblings would have been riding shotgun, this could have constituted a particularly nasty turn of events.

Not to worry, though. One lost trig assignment and I never again forgot to release the foot feed in time.

Town driving was problematic, I admit, as I had to drive all the way through Royal to get to the high school, a distance of four or five blocks punctuated by stop signs at a corner or two. I've always been a person who takes the rule of law seriously.

Unfortunately, every time I drove my ill-equipped car, I violated the State of Iowa's Rules of the Road, since I couldn't obey those darned stop signs. But by timing my comings and goings so as to avoid traffic—a term that applies only with extraordinary looseness to a place like Royal—I never experienced so much as a close call with pedestrians, other drivers, or the town cop.

Bringing my vehicle to a halt in the general vicinity of the high school involved shutting off the engine as I passed Bethlehem Lutheran Church and coasting the last block. I took a carnival-ride right turn just before the school, and continued to coast until it seemed safe to turn my tires into the curb. Most times, that was enough to bring the car to a full stop without attracting much attention.

Obviously, for a bright, motivated high-schooler like I was, getting to school was a piece of cake. Getting home was a different matter, for the last quarter mile of our notoriously tricky driveway, involved climbing the steepest rise in all of Clay County.

Serious acceleration was required!

Initially, I couldn't get the hang of killing the engine in time to avoid careening into the farm yard with a dangerous degree of momentum. Serendipitously, Dad had situated the large pile of straw and hay bales that wouldn't fit into our hay mow midway between the barn and the house. Having no suitable alternative, I executed a crash landing into the middle of the stack. Neither the car nor the hay seemed any the worse for it.

Problem solved!

Following the publication of her story in the anthology *Make Hay While the Sun Shines*, **Deb Kaczmarek** succumbed to irrational optimism and bought a small acreage near Webster, Minnesota, where she and her husband, Duane, raise chickens and swat mosquitoes.

Photo provided by Grover Reiser

Photo provided by George Gilbert

THE HEIRLOOM RING

George Gilbert

It had belonged to my great-grandmother. No one in the family knew for sure when she'd first come to have the diamond ring, but family legend had it that she brought it with her when, as a nervous sixteen year old, she'd traveled to the United States from Ireland to work as a domestic for a rich family in New York.

Maybe her mother had given it to her. We just didn't know. The ring was a plain gold band with a single half-karat diamond, not perfect, but the only thing of value she possessed. When she married, at age twenty-five, Amelia and her husband, August, moved from New York to Minnesota and started a family.

Amelia eventually passed the ring down to her oldest daughter, Evelyn, my grandmother. And from Grandma Evelyn it went to her only daughter, Florence—my mother. The tradition would have continued, but alas, my parents had only sons. That's how the ring came to be in my possession.

I could tell, when my mother gave the diamond ring to me, on my twenty-first birthday, she was hesitant to do so. But all she said was "Make sure it stays in the family, Georgie."

And that was my intention. Really. When I met Helen, I fell instantly in love. She was a vibrant redhead, lovely, and smart.

We were married, and naturally I gave her the heirloom ring. We agreed that someday it would be passed down to our daughter.

But we didn't have a daughter. What we had instead was a bitter divorce. When I told Helen I wanted the ring back, she refused to give it over.

"It was a gift, and you don't take back gifts," she told me with the arrogance I'd once loved about her but eventually grew to despise. "I didn't ask you to give back the golf clubs, did I?"

"It's hardly the same thing," I said. She refused to listen to reason.

In the division of property I fought to get the ring back, but even my lawyer didn't hold out much hope. My losing the ring broke my mother's heart. There was nothing to do but move on. I married again, and my wife and I had four daughters. The irony was not lost on me.

I didn't see Helen again for nearly thirty-five years. She left Minnesota, and I heard she'd also married again. There was no reason for us to stay in touch. All we had in common were a few memories, some happy, most not so much.

When we did bump into each other again, enough time had passed that the old hostilities no longer seemed so important. The years had been kind to Helen. She was as pretty as ever. Her hair was still red, though shorter, and she'd kept her figure. At the retirement party for her uncle, whose son was still a friend of mine, our eyes met across the crowded banquet hall. To my surprise, Helen came over and gave me a brief hug.

"It's good to see you, George," she said, looking like she meant it.

My eyes went to her left hand. There was no ring. I didn't bring it up.

We talked through the evening. A few people at the party gave us curious looks, especially when Helen and I danced together, but we hardly noticed. My wife had passed away the year before, and Helen told me she'd been widowed nearly ten years earlier. I hadn't heard that.

"Stan was a wonderful man," Helen told me as the party was winding down. "I'm afraid I wasn't always easy on him."

"Imagine that," I said, and we both laughed.

She looked down at her hands. "I still have it, you know."

I pretended not to know what she was talking about. I didn't want anything to spoil the evening.

She wasn't going to let me off that easy. "I was wrong not to give you back your grandmother's ring."

"My great-grandmother's ring," I couldn't help saying.

Helen smiled, and I saw again the girl I'd fallen in love with. She told me the ring was in her bag at the hotel, and she would bring it to me the next day. We arranged to meet for coffee in the morning.

And meet we did. For coffee, which turned into lunch. She had brought the ring with her, as promised, but somehow I never got around to taking it.

Six months later, when I married Helen for the second time, she wore the diamond ring on her left hand. She said she wanted to wear it for a little while longer, but promised we would give it to my oldest daughter.

I'm not worried.

George Gilbert lives in Minnesota, where he teaches math to middle-schoolers, a task that makes his tumultuous early marriage seem like a picnic.

Photos provided by Joyce Jenkins

WHEN MEMORIES BECOME A TREASURE

Joyce Jenkins

On June 23rd 1950, our first child was born. When I heard, "It's a girl," I was overjoyed. What I didn't hear anyone say is, "She's beautiful and all is fine."

When I saw her for the first time she was listless, and I could tell there was something not right. We named her Rhonda Sue.

The day before we were discharged from the hospital, the doctor told me Rhonda had a respiratory problem and wasn't taking nourishment. He made an appointment for her in Sioux City, for tests and observation.

After three days, Warren and I got a call that we could come and take our baby home. We left Sioux City with a grim outlook, following the doctor's report that Rhonda's brain had not fully developed, and she might not live beyond six months. He also said if she did live beyond the optimistic six months, there was the probability she would never walk or talk and would require constant, specialized care.

The doctor encouraged us to institutionalize her before we became too attached. It was a decision that was not easy to face or to make. My mom and dad promised they would help us care for Rhonda, and they never broke their promise. They were a source of strength during a very difficult time, as we decided to keep Rhonda at home.

Institutionalizing Rhonda had not, for us, been an option, but at times it was hard not to reconsider. Instead, we found alternatives. A close friend recommended a chiropractor in Milford who could possibly help with Rhonda's physical development.

For several months, with Mom and Dad, we made the trip to Milford twice a week, even in the worst of weather. Rhonda showed improvement, becoming more active and alert. With her continued progress I was more determined than ever not to give up.

The same friend also told us of a spiritual healer in Everly, and we added that option to Rhonda's developmental regimen. From the chiropractic treatments to the rituals of the spiritual healer, I found the hope that Rhonda was on her way to developing to her full potential.

I traveled with friends to Sunrise Ranch, in Loveland Colorado, a spiritual retreat center. Being there was a harmonious experience for me, and with the special prayers being said for Rhonda, I felt the healing powers of that place being transferred to her.

As Rhonda approached her second birthday she'd begun trying to feed herself, and was pulling herself up to stand. With continued encouragement and help, she also tried to take a few tentative steps. After many failed attempts to walk, she suddenly took off on her own. We were amazed and overjoyed.

Rhonda's first word was "accun" or ice-cream to all of us. Accun was an association she made with my father. When he would come to visit, he always brought ice cream, and Rhonda would greet him with her word.

To Rhonda accun meant ice cream. For us, it meant "miracle." Our prayers were being answered. Simply not giving up was proving to be an effective treatment.

My parents were always present with support and encouragement. To Grandma and Grandpa, Rhonda was their little girl and she spent a lot of time with them.

Rodney and Karen, our other two children, made our family complete. The three children were close, but as their school activities and my job took more and more time, Rhonda spent more time with her grandparents, and eventually she made her home with them. They lived nearby, so we were never out of touch with them and with Rhonda.

My mom and dad's constant attention helped Rhonda, and she continued to improve and develop beyond anyone's expectations. Her vocabulary expanded at an unbelievable rate.

Rhonda was afflicted with many health and behavioral issues throughout her life. There were trying challenges to endure, but we faced them head-on and never surrendered our commitment to unconditionally love and care for her. The health issues persisted, but in time, behavioral medications helped to manage many of the problems.

After my dad passed away, Grandma continued to care for Rhonda.

Village Northwest has a workshop in Sheldon for mentally and physically disabled individuals. Rhonda traveled there daily. Grandma made sure she got on the bus in the mornings and was always there to meet her in the evening.

Once, while at the Village, Rhonda had a bad fall on the ice and broke her hip. After that Grandma could no longer fulfill the role as her caregiver, and Rhonda moved back home with Warren and me. The transition was devastating for Grandma, something I would not fully understand until much later, when I found myself in a similar situation.

The time Rhonda spent at home offered many joys and blessings, as well as lifelong lessons and impressionable memories. Rhonda and her dad were the best of buddies. He contributed a large part to the responsibility of her care, and made it possible for me to continue working. The two would spend summer afternoons sitting outside to pass the time, and she picked up his habit of making straightforward and amusing comments that made me laugh, but were sometimes also embarrassing. She was certainly her father's daughter.

Through different social programs Rhonda was able to get out more in the community. It was an exciting time for her, being able to meet different people and socialize with others outside the family. Going out for a cup of coffee and a cookie, visiting with those who would stop to say hi, spending an entire afternoon at the library where she picked out children's books and flipped through the pages of every book that caught her interest, and eating out—these were just a few of the simple pleasures she looked forward to.

I was extremely grateful for these services, as they were not only beneficial for Rhonda, but also allowed me some free time while she was out with the trusted professionals. Volunteers from our church came once a week to read Bible stories to her from Sunday school lessons. She learned about Jesus, and they taught her how to pray.

After Rhonda's dad passed away, it became more difficult for me to care for her. I realized the day was approaching when once again I would be faced with a difficult decision regarding her care.

This decision was made for me, however, when Rhonda suffered a stroke and lost the use of her right arm and leg. There was only one option, and that was to place her in a nursing home. I was terrified at the thought of how she would accept this significant change to her life, but it was a surprise and a tremendous relief when she adapted well to her new surroundings.

Once again, Rhonda showed her resilience. The staff and residents at the Community Memorial Health Center in Hartley adopted her into their family, making her feel welcome and secure. Only once did she ask me to take her home. When I explained to her why I could no longer care for her there, she never asked again. The reality was something we both had to accept. I looked forward to going to see her every day. Seeing her happy, well adjusted, and getting the best of care was all I could ask for.

Then Rhonda suffered a second stroke, leaving her unable to speak or swallow. She lost two of the things she loved most in life—talking and eating. During the week that followed, we witnessed her struggle to express herself, wanting so much to speak, eat, and drink. As we stood by her side, we could see that she was terrified, unable to understand what was happening to her.

With all the obstacles and challenges she had overcome in her life, this was one we knew she would not be able to conquer. As the end drew near, with her family and pastor by her side, a spiritual comfort came over all of us. As Pastor recited Rhonda's favorite prayer, "Now I Lay Me Down to Sleep," and finally closing with ". . . if I should die before I wake, I pray the Lord my soul to take," Rhonda took her last breath.

In that moment we knew she was with Jesus. He had taken her to a better place, where she was joining her loved ones who waited for her to join them in Heaven.

Because of Rhonda's dependence on me, I had long wished the Lord would take her before me. That wish was granted on September 18th, 2010.

During her sixty years, Rhonda touched many lives with the unique love, kindness, and compassion she showed to everyone she knew. She left our family with a sense of pride in having known her, and her astonishing development left me with a strong belief that there is power in prayer and persistence.

Rhonda's extraordinary ability to love unconditionally, her selfless kindness, her innocence, her sense of humor, and her keen memory were evidence that she truly had developed beyond what anyone had expected or dared hope.

Rhonda was more than a miracle. She was a gift. Everything she gave came from her heart. In return, she needed only to know she would never be alone, that she was loved, and she would always be cared for. To have known her is to believe that people really are put on this earth for a special purpose. She did more than just deliver her purpose, she lived it.

I think of her daily, and cherish the priceless memories she left behind.

Memories that are now a treasure.

Joyce Jenkins dedicates "When Memories Become a Treasure" to the memory of Rhonda, her special-needs daughter, who touched many lives in many ways; and to her parents, who gave many years of their wholehearted support. Joyce was born in 1922 in Hartley, Iowa, where she still resides. She has one son, another daughter and one grandson. She lives a full life and is thankful for her friends and family.

Photo provided by Janet Branson

A TRUNKFUL OF MEMORIES

Janet Branson

A few years ago my grandson Drew, seven at the time, his sister, and two of his cousins came to visit for a few days. It was the first time he'd been to our house, so the first thing he did was explore the yard and the house.

When he came to my bedroom, he spotted my grandmother's steamer trunk. His eyes got big. "Grandma, is that a treasure chest?"

"Well, yes. I guess you could call it that," I told him. "It has some of my treasures in it from a long time ago."

"What kinds of treasures?"

"I think you're going to have to wait a day or two until we have time to look."

Neither he nor his sister and cousins had the patience to wait to see what was in the treasure chest, but they managed. Finally the day came. We opened it.

"Oh, Grandma! What are these little clothes here on top?" asked Melissa.

"Those are clothes that your daddies and your uncles wore when they were babies," I explained, picking up a small outfit. "I made this blue shirt and diaper cover for David when he was tiny. Here's the little Santa pajamas we brought Jeff home in from the hospital. He came home on Christmas Eve." I held up another one. "Look at this little cream sweater and booties. Your

Great-grandma Branson knitted this for him. Isn't it beautiful? He never wore it. I was afraid he'd spit up on it. I wish now I'd let him wear it."

"Oh! What's this?" asked Mikayla, reaching in and picking up a very small blue garment.

"Oh, my!" I exclaimed. "This is the doll sweater-set that Mrs. Santa crocheted for me one Christmas when I was four or five. I remember the doll it came with. She was very pretty, with two pearly-white teeth. She disappeared a long time ago. I didn't know I still had the little sweater-set. And here's the little yellow suit your Uncle Gary wore in a wedding when he was about seven. Isn't it cute?"

"Eew!" squealed Drew.

"The truth is, Uncle Gary didn't like that suit very much either," I whispered. "Here are two skirts that I wore in high school. My mother made these. Look at the wonderful pleats in this yellow print skirt. And this black dress with the painted flowers on the skirt was one of my favorites when I was in college. The flower on the bodice looks like a corsage."

I continued to sift through the clothes in the steamer trunk.

"Oh, look . . . here's the dress I wore to the senior banquet when I was seventeen. It has a gathered white taffeta skirt with a sheer flowered overlay and matching three-quarter sleeved jacket. And here's another party dress I wore in college. I loved its puffy sleeves." The dress was a light-blue satin brocade with a sheer layer of blue nylon over it. "All these full skirts were worn over two or three full layers of can cans," I told them.

I lifted out another colorful garment.

"I'd forgotten I still had this dress," I said, holding it up for them to see. "This was the pioneer dress I made for the Hartley Bicentennial the summer of 1979. I wore a hoop skirt under it. I only had two or three opportunities to wear this dress, but I loved it. It made me feel like a real southern belle."

"Oh, Grandma, these dresses are so pretty," said Dani. "Do you think we could try them on?"

The girls were ten, eleven and fourteen, so I said, "Yes, I think that would be fun."

Drew wasn't interested in trying on clothes.

After the girls changed into the dresses, they modeled them for Grandpa and we took pictures for them to show their parents.

Later, as I thought about that fun afternoon, I began to remember some of the other clothes I'd worn in my youth. In that era, all the girls wore dresses to school. I had a little gray dress with a yellow and gray plaid collar, and a matching ruffle around the skirt. I wore it for my first grade class picture. That was about the time Mom took me shopping in the Hart-Albin department store and bought a little navy blue cape with a print lining. I loved wearing it.

In the spring when I was in third grade, my mother made a white print dress and bought a new pair of white sandals for me to wear to the city-wide school Spring Festival.

It was such an exciting event. Each class did something different. Our class marched around in a circle to a recording of a Sousa march. I was very excited, as I'd never had sandals before. You should have seen me march in them! It was like they had springs in the soles.

Daddy didn't like them, however. He didn't think they were good for my feet. He'd rather I had some brown oxfords to wear. Proper supportive footwear, you know. What do daddies know?

I grew up on the farm. We weren't poor, we just didn't have much money. Mom was very good at stretching a dollar. When I was in fifth grade she learned of a lady who had some girls' clothing for sale, and we went to see her. Mom chose two wool pleated skirts. Afterward she said we could go to Penny's to buy sweaters and matching socks to wear with them. I was puzzled by this. I'd never had sweaters. I wondered if they'd make me sweat, or what.

One year, when I was ten or eleven, Mom made a new Easter dress for me. It was yellow with a full skirt and a dropped waist.

I had to stand up on the kitchen table so she could mark the hem. Around and around I turned until she got it just right. Oh, how I hated that process. My legs would itch, my face twitched, my feet turned numb, but I had to stand still while she pinned up the skirt. That was the bad part of having a new dress made, but this time it was even worse, because I never even liked that dress.

Usually Mom made my clothes, but for my eighth grade graduation in 1955 she took me to the Vaughn-Ragsdale department store for a dress. We chose an iridescent, light mauve dress with a winged collar, dropped waist and a full skirt. It was expensive, costing fourteen dollars.

About the same time, a neighbor lady gave me a black pleated satin-like skirt with matching jacket. The jacket had sheer sleeves and a double layer of fabric in the front and back, embroidered with silver in a floral design and a tie bow at the neck. It was a hand-me-down, but I thought it was beautiful, and Mom bought an expensive six-dollar white nylon blouse to go with it. I wore that outfit to church for several years.

One of my favorite dresses was a turquoise and cream "squaw dress" that Mom made for me when I was a sophomore. They were all the rage at the time. My dress was made of a type of wrinkled material. The skirt had three gathered tiers, with the cream tier in the center. The bodice was turquoise with three-quarter sleeves, and the entire dress was trimmed in black and pink rickrack with a silver thread running through it. Several rows decorated the sleeves, collar and bodice, and on each tier of the skirt. It was very full and, of course, I wore it over several layers of stiffly starched can-cans. A silver butterfly Concho-belt completed the outfit, which I wore all through high school. I sometimes wonder what happened to that dress.

My favorite Easter dress was one we bought the spring I turned sixteen. We paid sixteen dollars for it. It was white with little blue flowers all over, sleeveless, with a navy bolero jacket and a navy "duster," which was like a coat but without a lining. I also bought my first pair of two-inch heels to wear with it. In another year I would be wearing three-inch spiked heels.

What fun it was to explore the depths of my grandmother's trunk, all the while digging into my memory bank! The grandchildren thoroughly enjoyed it.

Next time they come, I think we'll open it again. We should also take down the big box from the top of my closet that contains my wedding gown. The girls will really enjoy trying that on, and I'd love it too.

Janet Branson has lived in Hartley, Iowa, for forty-six years. She began writing several years ago when she retired as a school cook. Her main focus is on stories from her childhood, and genealogy, in the hope that her children will find them interesting. She's grandmother to twelve beautiful children who are the light of her life.

Photo provided by Janet Branson

Photo provided by Betty Taylor

GRANDPA'S COTTAGE

Lisa Nehring

I woke to the damp summer smell of cinder block. The "walls," pocketed sheets strung on wire to make two bedrooms out of one, billowed softly as Grandpa came to wake me. The sun was new and pale at 5 a.m. We were going fishing!

I slipped on shorts and a T-shirt and used the facilities, a tiny cubicle off the bedrooms that contained a toilet, sink and hanging light bulb. Nothing fancy, but everything anyone needed. I loved the cottage and summer days spent there!

Grandma and Grandpa had farmed for decades, and they had the stories and battle scars to prove it. They survived through faith, yearly winter trips to Florida, and frequent use of their lake cottage, a simple cinder block rectangle, hand built by my Dad and Grandpa in the '50s.

Uncle Earl, one of Grandpa's younger brothers and just as grey and youthful as Grandpa, "owned" the lake. I was never really sure what that meant, other than he seemed to know everyone, and my sisters and I were treated like royalty by the other summer folk.

"Oh, you're Lloyd's grandkids," they'd shout when we'd point out the cottage from the middle of the lake.

My older sister, Sue, and I would canoe for hours in the rushes, pretending to be Indians. We were both excellent swimmers, thanks to the lake and Dad's "do or drown" approach to swimming lessons. Apparently our survival skills kicked in and we swam, as evidenced by the fact that he hadn't lost a kid yet to his method.

As a result, we threw our life jackets into the middle of the canoe as soon as we were out of site of the cottage. If our younger sister, Kristie, tagged along, we'd make her keep her life jacket on. We trusted our own ability, but there was no way we were going to have her drowning on our watch. Our survival skills extended beyond sink or swim to include keeping Kristie alive and well.

Afternoons found us playing croquet on the large, luxuriously grassy area between the cottage and the lake. Grandma held the mallet in her right hand, in front of her, instead of between her legs. After taking several test swings, she'd hit with deadly accuracy. She felt no remorse at sending a novice granddaughter's ball into Uncle Earl's yard next door, or within inches of the lake. She drew steadily ahead while the rest of us lagged behind. We'd laugh because we knew we didn't stand a chance against her.

Inevitably, someone sat the game out. They'd choose instead to swing lazily amongst the branches of the giant willow in the tree swing, serenaded by the buzzing of dragonflies and croquet balls being walloped out of bounds.

Evenings often found us next door, singing for Uncle Earl's wife, Dolly. She was sickly and frail, with bright red rouge on her cheeks and paper-thin skin. Her house smelled like roses. We'd sing rounds and church hymns, and she'd listen as raptly as though we were the Mormon Tabernacle Choir.

Later, Uncle Earl would usher us over to his pontoon boat and host us on a long, leisurely pontoon ride around the lake. My sisters and I, six legs dangling, sat at the front of the boat. We'd scare the fishes and revel in the summer sounds of the lake.

At 5:10 a.m. Grandpa and I headed out to the middle of the lake. The bait and pail sat in the middle of the old aluminum rowboat. He'd hook the worm and I'd hold the bamboo pole.

A bite! And there was Grandpa, taking the fish off the hook. I was pole holder extraordinaire and happy company, and that was good enough for him. He shooshed me every now and then, so I wouldn't scare the fish.

Grandpa loved us all, but I was pretty sure I was his favorite. I liked being with him, despite the funny white hair growing out of his ears. He was gentle and firm and patiently explained things to me.

Finally our fish pail was full, and Grandma had promised fried fish for breakfast. I wasn't too sure about the menu, but cooking was Grandma's craft so I was willing to give it a shot.

We rowed back to the short pier in front of the cottage and walked across the lawn, the early morning dew soaking our sneakers.

Across the road, in front of Uncle Earl's huge metal storage barn, was a chopping block. Grandpa gutted out the fish. I watched while he explained scaling and boning and filleting. Grandpa told me what a great watcher I was and I knew he meant it, even if he was the one doing all the dirty work.

Grandma breaded and fried the whole "mess of 'em." She served them up steaming hot crunchy, with cold milk from the icebox and homemade apple pie. It was a magical breakfast feast, served while the day was still simple and sweet.

That night we played board games. Three card tables were set up in the L-shaped area from the kitchen to the living room. Aunt Carrie, grandpa's baby sister, and her rotund husband, my favorite Uncle Gay, came over to play Rook and Aggravation and Chinese checkers.

Grandma was queen of the kitchen, queen of the croquet field and queen of cards. She hardly ever spoke, but her focused determination dominated the games. The rest of us knew we didn't stand a chance if she was at our table, but we reveled in the competition, which was made sweeter by candy dishes set out with M & Ms, hard candy and peanuts. And, of course, her homemade pies were a constant fixture on the tidy counter.

Grandma's cooking was done with the same quiet determination as her game playing. None of us doubted for a minute that she was known throughout the county for her cooking. She was certainly a legend among us girls, and we reminisced throughout the year about homemade egg noodles and baked goods.

Knowing she'd win at any game was a small price to pay in exchange for the twice-yearly foray into carbohydrate heaven.

Dad would forgo sweets in favor of his favorite treat, pickled eggs. Whole, hard-boiled eggs, pickled with beets and canned. The color was a lovely pastel pink, the smell pure, unadulterated vinegar. Grandma would beam as Dad ate whole egg after whole egg, followed by the beets, finishing with the pink vinegary pickle juice. He'd roll his eyes and "Mmm" with appreciation. Grandma would chuckle and say, "Now, now," but she was at her happiest then.

Crickets chirruped through open windows and Grandma's stained glass lamp glowed. Folks around the tables laughed or groaned, depending on how well their turn had gone. And soon, the games had ended and the last piece of pie was eaten.

Hugs, the German kind that knocked the breath out of us, were part of the evening ritual. My sisters and I were the only grandkids, and we were treasured. We were part of their tribe, and being young, the future. They hugged and kissed us, their hazel eyes shining, holding our faces in their hands and would tell us how proud they were of us. And we would wonder why. We were, after all, just regular kids.

Everyone agreed the cottage was a great idea, built for long summer vacations of cards and canoeing and croquet. Surrounded by family, my sisters and I didn't fully appreciate the importance of those days until much later.

Grandma and Grandpa are long gone, and the aunts and uncles. Mom and my older sister, Sue, and Dad, just this year, passed away, too.

My little sister, the one we kept from drowning all those years ago, called after looking through Dad's scrapbooks, and asked did I want the one with the pictures of the cottage, the one with the pictures of Grandma and Grandpa and the aunts and uncles?

Choking back tears, full of happy memories of being loved, and of loss, I said, "I do."

Lisa Nehring grew up in the Midwest and has spent her adult life living coast to coast, raising her five children in several states. When not writing or blogging, she's gardening, reading, homeschooling and porch-sitting with her husband. More of her writing can be seen at www.goldengrasses.blogspot.com.

GRANDPA'S TRACTOR

Karen Schwaller

It was a familiar place; more familiar to some than to others. I lived there for my first eighteen years, but my parents had lived there for more than fifty years. On this day, pickup trucks lined the gravel road. I could smell the aroma from the lunch wagon. I could see people in bib overalls and greasy jeans milling about. I could hear the hiss of a John Deere Model A being started as well as the starting rumble of the other tractors lined up in the yard.

It was the day of my parents' farm sale.

Farm sale day is a day unlike any other in the life of a farmer and his family. A rite of passage, painful as it may be. My family traveled to the Remsen-Kingsley area to be part of a day that held the possibility of great things for our two boys. They had saved money all summer, and wanted nothing more than to get one of Grandpa's tractors.

For my dad, going to farm sales was something he had done often in his seventy-four years. But this sale was his, and his sorrow showed the night before the sale as his family gathered to look around the farm and share stories, laughter and tears. A farmer becomes one with the land and the work it takes. Letting go of those things used each day was so hard. The place had once been a thriving farm with lots of kids and lots of work to be done. But on that night a lifetime of sweat and grit was lined up and ready to be sold to the highest bidder.

Before the crowd arrived and the hum of the auctioneer began, my dad and I walked around the items lined up all around the yard. I wondered how he ever used all that stuff, as he gazed at it through misty, nostalgic eyes, remembering, and wondering how fifty years of farming could have possibly gone by so quickly.

He bent over to show me an item, and as he did one of his tears splashed onto it. I felt a lump in my throat, and when the auctioneer began, I realized it was all really happening.

It was quite a feeling at first, seeing three of my four brothers on the flat racks with the auctioneer, holding up parts of their own farm memories for the bidders to see, then handing things over to new owners. They had worked hard with our dad, with all of it, and they had also worked hard to get it ready to sell.

Finally it was time to sell the farm equipment. Our sons had stomachaches, worried that there were plenty of other bidders out there who had more money than they. But no other bidders had more desire to own one of Grandpa's tractors than those two boys on that day.

The first tractor, a John Deere A, sold to my oldest brother.

I told him, "It's really cool you got that tractor."

As he replied, "Well, it's been here fifty years," he began to choke up.

It used to amaze me, as a kid, to watch Dad and my brothers start that tractor. I'd thought it positively mystifying to see them turn the flywheel by hand to get it started.

Other tractors and equipment sold, including an older Honda motorcycle one of our sons purchased. Soon it was time to sell the tractor our boys wanted, an Oliver 1750, the only tractor that my father had ever bought brand new. Grandpa Art's farm was the only home that tractor had ever known.

The boys had set their top price and stood nervously beside their dad as he did the bidding for them. As the bidding went on, they soon neared their top-end price. They bid yet another time and another. Soon their dad could see it would go too far over their price, and shook his head sadly as he looked at the boys. He knew how much they wanted that tractor.

I felt their disappointment. It showed on their faces, and probably on my own. The bidding continued, but then, as if a miracle had occurred, the man who was bidding against our sons somehow figured out that grandsons were bidding on the tractor, and he backed off.

The auctioneer cried, "Sold!" as he had so many times that day, then came over and shook our sons' hands, congratulating them on becoming the proud new owners of one of Grandpa Art's most beloved tractors.

The boys were overcome with joy, as were many there in that moment. Tears flowed, by family members and friends of all ages. The auctioneer later told me he had to look away because he was afraid he would start crying, too. Many hands clapped, sharing in our happiness and relief, and cheers went out for a tractor that went to two young farmers who had fallen in love with it, simply because it was one of their grandpa's tractors.

The tractor was loaded up on a trailer and taken to its new home, with yellow and black streamers, placed on it by our sons' very happy aunts, billowing from it.

The next night the boys and I sat down to e-mail my youngest brother in Arkansas to let him know they had purchased Grandpa's tractor. My husband said, "Why don't you tell the rest of the story, guys?"

Looking sheepishly at me, one of them said, "We broke the headlight out on the motorcycle."

I knew he was speaking of the older Honda they had just bought at the auction. "How did that happen already?" I inquired.

After a pause, he replied, "I hit the 1750. We're not used to the throttle yet."

It felt really good to laugh.

Karen Schwaller is a farm wife, mother and freelance writer from Milford, Iowa. She grew up on a farm in northwest Iowa, but did most of her learning about farm life after she married her husband, Dave, and while together raising their three children. The Oliver 1750 tractor, affectionately known as "Grandpa's Tractor," has become an even more treasured gem to her family since Grandpa Art (Schroeder) died in 2009, just three years after the farm sale.

Sketch by LaVonne M. Hansen

THE SURPRISE

Verla Klaessy

The soft glow of the gas ceiling lamp enlarged the shadows in the corner. My dad and I were playing a game of checkers on the kitchen table. It was the end of winter and tufts of grass were peeking through the dirt in the yard. Mother was in a rocker darning socks, a never-ending job. The Motorola radio had signed off from a musical program, and *Fibber McGee and Molly* would soon start.

I was especially fond of the Aladdin lamp sitting on a table in the dining room. It was lit only on special occasions. A square-shaped kerosene lamp that could be carried was what we used more often as we moved from room to room. Sometimes candles were lit.

There were a few red embers in the old wood burning Majestic cookstove, and the teakettle had been filled for the morning coffee. Mother had emptied the wash pan that sat under the icebox. It held the drippings from the chunk of block ice the ice man had brought that morning.

It was a comfortable time of the day, with chores done, the milk separated and dishes washed. We gathered around the radio for an hour or so of laughter before bedtime.

Watching my dad climb on a chair to change the gas mantles on the overhead light was fascinating to an eight year old. Most of our reading was done in daylight, but it was a good feeling to have a light in the dim evening darkness. Our neighbors also lit their lamps in the evening.

I did not visit my grandparents in town often, but when I did I marveled at the bright lights in every room and up the curving stairway, all provided by electricity. I assumed only the rich could afford it.

My dad carried a kerosene lantern out to the barn to feed the animals and milk the cows when it was dark. I would look out the kitchen window and watch for his light swinging back and forth as he returned to the house for supper.

At bedtime the stairs up to my bedroom were very dark, but most of the time one of my parents would lead the way with the kerosene lamp held high. In my room was a miniature lamp, similar to the big one. It also held kerosene and would be lit to show a tiny flicker until I crawled into bed. Then Mother would blow it out.

Sometimes, if the weather was warm, we sat on the front porch to look at the bright stars overhead, brilliant in the ink-black darkness of the night sky. Fireflies would dart above the grass, and we giggled with delight as we tried to catch them to put them into a jar. When we'd caught enough, we held the jar up as a kind of lantern in the dark.

Then one day a curious thing happened. Huge trucks with long poles drove down our gravel road and stopped near our farmhouse. I had no idea how electricity actually got to a house, so I was eager to watch as the poles were lowered into holes near the ditch on the edge of our field. When the wires were strung from pole to pole, even my folks seemed excited and told me one day we would have lights like my grandpa and grandma had.

The truck pulled into our farmyard and a huge pole was put in the center of the outer yard. Wires were run to the house and to the barn. It was taking a long time, as all the neighbors were also getting their poles installed.

When it was time for school to begin again in the fall, nothing was finished. We still used the same lamps and lanterns.

And then one day, when I hurried home, my dad was waiting for me at the back door.

"Come see the surprise," he said.

As I entered the kitchen, I saw that the globe with the gas mantle was gone. In its place was a single light bulb, with a string hanging down.

Dad told me to give it a pull, which I did. I blinked my eyes as a bright light shone in my face. "We have 'lectricity," I squealed, and we all did a little dance around the kitchen.

Then I ran upstairs to my bedroom. Sure enough, there was another string hanging below a bare light bulb in the ceiling. I had my very own 'lectricity!

Little did I know what was to follow. We replaced our ice box with a refrigerator; the kerosene stove with a hot plate; and the irons heated on the cookstove were replaced by an electric iron. The new washing machine had an electric motor, and the fan on the furnace blew warm air through the rooms.

Bare bulbs with magnificent shades became lights of beauty. A vacuum cleaner was a delight to use for cleaning, as well as to scare younger children who had never seen one.

Over the years nearly all things eventually became electric. Today, if the power goes off for a few minutes or an hour there is panic, as nothing works; the garage door opener, the washer and dryer, the TV, the computer—all are dependent on electricity. With no lights, the rooms are dark.

Now I can sit at my computer and read email from France, Botswana, the Philippines, and all parts of the Western Hemisphere. I may turn on a lamp with a clap, a touch or a voice. Automatic has become a way of life as doors open and close with the "electric eye." A microwave oven cooks our food with the push of a button and doctors see the insides of our bodies with MRIs, CAT scans and X-rays.

Great advancements have been made since the year 600 AD, when static electricity was discovered by rubbing an amber stone with animal fur. Many experiments were to follow, by Ben Franklin, Thomas Edison and the many developers since.

I think we take this great miracle for granted and view it as commonplace. But could we ever do without it again?

Verla Klaessy, a great-grandmother of three, recalls growing up on a farm in the 1930s. Living on the fleeting edge of pioneer life to present day technology has been the best time period ever experienced.

Sketch provided by Karen Schutt

BESSIE MAE MOOCHO

Karen Jones Schutt

Bessie Mae Moocho* was evil. She didn't like people, didn't like the other cows, or even the lush pasture with plenty of water and shade. She was mean, from her large bony head to her hard-hitting tail.

When Dad first saw her, she was standing meekly in a pen at the sale barn. With eyes lowered demurely, she showed all the signs of being a good and gentle milk cow. True, she was tall and raw-boned, but she was part Holstein, and Holsteins are known to be large, yet mild-mannered. Dad assumed I would be able to milk her with no trouble.

After she arrived home and was unloaded into the pasture, she immediately charged toward Lillian, Aggie, and Geraldine. Those three small Jersey-Guernsey mix cows took off for the far corner of the pasture and huddled together while Bessie Mae drank her fill at the water tank, then munched her way to the shade of the big maple tree.

It became established that Bessie Mae was the boss of Lillian, Aggie, and Geraldine. She was the first in the barn, the first at the water tank, and the first to find any weak place in the fence to escape into the cornfield.

When that happened, Dad was usually around to help corral her back to the pasture, while the other three cows seemed to watch her bad behavior in disbelief. With Dad hollering invectives, she would gallop to the broken fence and back into the pasture. Then she would turn and glare at Dad as if to say it was his fault the fence was weak in the first place.

It was my brother Gary's job to put the four cows in the barn for milking and give them their grain. One day he went to Dad complaining that Bessie Mae was standing in the water tank and wouldn't let Lillian, Aggie, and Geraldine drink before heading for the barn.

"Well, yell at her, show her who's boss," growled Dad.

"I did, but she won't move."

Dad said something under his breath, picked up a handy 2 x 4 and started for Bessie Mae.

She must have recognized the look in his eyes, not to mention the 2 x 4, because she nimbly stepped from the tank. Without a backward glance, she ambled to the barn and her stanchion, and began eating her grain.

I usually had no trouble milking Bessie Mae, provided I fastened the kickers around her legs and tied up her tail. The kickers were not to protect me, but to keep her from tipping over the milk pail, usually when it was about half full. It also helped that she was milked first, while still eating her grain.

One mid-July day, after a soaking rain, Dad announced that he and Mother were taking the day off to go to Sioux City and they wouldn't be home until late in the evening. Marilyn would be in charge and Gary and I were responsible for the chores.

"But, Bessie Mae will be naughty," I whined.

"All you have to do is make her understand you're the boss and you won't have any trouble."

"That's easier said than done," I muttered under my breath.

Gary and I watched Bessie Mae as the folks drove off the place and down the gravel road. She actually stopped grazing, lifted her head, and thoughtfully watched the car disappear over a hill. I knew she was plotting something.

"Gary," I said, "we should probably keep a close eye on Bessie Mae. She knows Dad is gone."

So, off and on during the day we checked on her. The four cows were always peacefully grazing and behaving themselves.

Marilyn made a lemon meringue pie, which was our standard noon meal when the folks were away. Gary and I rode our bikes and worked on the tree house, while often checking on the cows.

But, late in the afternoon, Gary reported breathlessly: "Bessie Mae, and Lillian, and Aggie, and Geraldine are all missing!"

We were on our bikes and out the driveway in no time. Standing together in the middle of the road were Lillian, Aggie, and Geraldine. They were plainly puzzled as to why they were there. If they could have spoken, one of them would have said, "Bessie Mae made us do it. We didn't want to leave the pasture."

We had no trouble driving them into the barn and their own personal stanchions. They seemed relieved to be there.

Now to deal with Bessie Mae. As Gary and I raced down the road again, we spied that wicked beast looking out from the cornfield. She was daring us to come after her.

"What shall we do?" I wondered.

"Let's just charge her," suggested Gary.

"But she'll chase us," I pointed out.

"Do you have a better idea?" he asked.

I didn't, so we each picked up broken corn stalks and charged toward her, shrieking and screaming. We waved those flimsy stalks over our heads as though they were dangerous weapons.

Bessie Mae must have decided we meant business, so she galloped off to the barn. Gary and I thought we had won the battle, but we were dealing with Bessie Mae, after all. Instead of heading for her stanchion, she ambled to the far end of the milking parlor, turned around and lowered her head. She was plainly daring me to come closer.

I knew I was defeated.

"Gary, have Marilyn call Carl. Bessie Mae will probably kill me if I get any closer."

Our neighbor Carl soon arrived. "Having a little trouble with Bessie Mae again?" he asked. All our neighbors were familiar with our ornery cow and most of them had helped us deal with her at one time or another.

"Yes," I answered. "She's being stubborn and won't go into her stanchion."

With that, Carl strode toward her, waving his arms and shouting, "HYAR! HAYR! Move it, you dumb cow!"

Of course, Bessie Mae walked meekly to her stanchion and began eating her grain.

"Do you want me to milk her, too?" he asked.

"I can milk her if you'll help me put on her kickers and tie up her tail," I replied.

"Where's the milk pail?" he asked.

We put up with Bessie Mae's cussedness until September. Then, one afternoon, we got off the bus to pandemonium in the cattle lot. Lillian, Aggie, and Geraldine were bawling their heads off. Bessie Mae was nowhere to be seen.

"Where is Bessie Mae?" we asked Mother.

"At the rendering plant, I hope," was her reply.

"Why? What happened?" I asked.

"Just go have a look at the garden."

With the three cows still bawling, we took a look at Mother's garden.

What we saw made our jaws drop in disbelief. The garden looked as though a tornado had churned through it. Tomatoes, cucumbers, and peppers were smashed and trampled. Winter squash were broken open. Carrots and onions were scattered over it all. It was a mess of Biblical proportion. Bessie Mae had certainly done a thorough job of ruining Mother's hard work and all that food.

By milking time, Lillian, Aggie, and Geraldine were still hollering about Bessie Mae. They had gotten used to her and her bossy ways.

Not much was said around the supper table. The loss of the garden and Bessie Mae were heavy on our minds. Dad casually mentioned that three cows were probably enough to handle now that harvest was about to begin.

We didn't miss Bessie Mae Moocho, but we had to admit she had brought excitement to the farm.

Dad never would say what he had done with Bessie Mae, but we suspected he took her back to the sale barn. We imagined her there, looking meek and demure, just waiting for her next victim. We hoped that whoever bought her lived a long, long way from our farm.

*Gary invented her name from a song popular of the time, "Bésame Mucho."

Karen Jones Schutt and her husband Charles have retired to the country near Sioux Falls, South Dakota. While there is not a Holstein cow for miles around, her garden provides tasty meals for the deer, rabbits and turkeys.

Photo provided by Judy Taber

HEAD 'EM UP! MOVE 'EM OUT!

Judy Taber

We opened the gate to the cattle lot and out spilled fifty-five mama cows with their calves at their sides, running to freedom. We headed them out the driveway and turned them south. The cattle drive was underway. While we might have looked like an episode of *Rawhide*, we were operating on a much smaller scale, as well as going a much shorter distance.

Rawhide was a television western set in the 1860s. It aired for eight seasons and portrayed the challenges faced by the men on a cattle drive. There were twenty to twenty-five riders to look after approximately three thousand head of cattle. The cattle drive began in San Antonio, Texas, and made its way along the Sedalia Trail. The final destination, Sedalia, is in Missouri about fifty miles east of Kansas City. The herd was estimated to be worth $50,000 to $60,000 when sold at market and represented a pool of cattle from approximately 200 owners.

In the late 1950s, my dad had a herd of stock cows made up of Hereford and Angus breeds that were kept for their meat. We raised the offspring to a market weight of eleven hundred to twelve hundred pounds, and then they were sold.

In the fall, after the corn was harvested, the cows were allowed the run of the farm to graze on cornstalks and glean any leftover ears of corn that had fallen off the stalks. It always amazed me that they could find anything out there to eat, but they did quite well for themselves. The young calves did their own grazing to supplement the milk they were still receiving from their mothers.

Before the herd was let out into our fields, we would move them to my Uncle Dale Taylor's farm to graze and glean in his harvested corn fields first. That involved driving the cows five and a half miles south on the gravel road and two and a quarter miles east on the A34 blacktop, which wasn't nearly as busy back then as it is now.

I was allowed to skip school to ride my horse, Kelly, and help. There were two of us on horses and two or three people in cars or pickups. Back then most of the farms were fenced in. Today it would be impossible to drive a herd of cattle down the road, as the fences have been removed.

We had to ride through the herd to get ahead of them so we could close any gates that were left open. We also stood watch at the intersections so the cows wouldn't turn and head down a side road.

Once the cows were past the gate or the intersection, we would ride through the herd again and set up watch at the next spot where they might escape. Invariably a few of them would test their luck and take off down a side road. I would turn Kelly and take chase. Thank goodness my horse ran faster than the cows. We would gallop past them, turn them around and head them back where they belonged.

Every herd has a cow that is a leader, or, as I like to call her, an instigator. Wherever that cow goes, the rest will follow. So we tried to make sure the instigator was heading in the direction we wanted them to go. Usually the rest would follow along.

Once the cows had tired from running in their initial burst of freedom, they walked quite agreeably. Vehicles that came up behind us were always a concern, however. Most of the time, the drivers were patient. If they were going to turn shortly, they would simply follow us until they came to their turn-off. Sometimes they would drive slowly through the herd and watch a gate or an intersection corner for us.

At last, we arrived at Uncle Dale's farm. Our next problem was getting the cows to turn through an open gate. For more than seven miles we had kept them going straight, and they wanted to continue to do so. But once the instigator cow was in the destination field, the rest of them followed and immediately began grazing.

The entire trip was completed by noon. The horses were loaded into our truck and hauled back to the farm, where Mom had noon dinner waiting. Then she drove me to school for afternoon classes.

After several weeks, when the cows had eaten everything that had nutritional value in the field we'd taken them to, we would reverse the process and bring the herd back home, heading west and north.

It was much colder by then and there was usually snow on the ground. I wasn't nearly as enthused about helping on the return trip. My hands got so cold that it was hard to hold the reins. We didn't have insulated coveralls back then, so I wore two pairs of pants and lots of layers to try to keep warm. When we were done, Mom always had hot chocolate ready to help me warm up.

The cows were content to be back home and settled in for the winter. The following fall we would do all of it again, and the excitement of the cattle drive would return.

Judy Taber, a retired adjunct university professor, and her husband, Gary, live in a home that they built on the south shore of Silver Lake at Lake Park, Iowa. Depending on the season and/or weather, she can be found working in her extensive gardens or creating stained and fused glass art.

Photo provided by Bonnie Ewoldt

SHOW CALVES

Bonnie Ewoldt

As a farm kid in the sixties, the highlight of every summer was the Crawford County Fair—a week of vacation without leaving home. Venders, carnival rides and the grandstand shows were exciting, but my favorite place to hang out was the cattle barn. From sunrise until late into the evening, for one week in July, I lived at the fair with my show calves.

But the lion's share of the work involved with showing cattle took place during the summer, before opening day.

Dad raised purebred Angus, so I always entered two or three heifers in the 4-H Calf and Cattle Show. The weeks leading up to the fair were hectic as I fought the heifers and broke them to lead.

The wild process began with halters. Since they'd spent their entire lives roaming free in the pasture, they weren't keen on the idea of having leather straps placed behind their ears and around their faces. I started the process by slipping a halter ever-so-slowly over a calf's head while its nose was in the feed trough.

One wrong move could spook it, causing it to back away and leaving me to wait patiently until it calmed down enough to return to the feed—so I could start over.

Eventually, they allowed me to slip halters on and off with no problem while it nonchalantly chomped away at the feed. When the time finally came that it didn't mind their halters, I left them in place all the time so they became accustomed to being haltered before moving on to the next step in the training.

The real work then began when I introduced the lead rope, an eight-foot-long piece of hemp line clipped to a chain on the halter, under each heifer's chin. This eventually gave me command of the animal, but *getting* command of an animal wasn't all that easy—a skinny high school girl was no match for hundreds of pounds of bovine muscle and determination! It was a battle of wills that started with tying the lead rope to the bunk and carefully clipping it to the halter.

The heifers were always shocked when they finished eating, tried to back away, and discovered themselves being held captive. They exploded! Raging, they bucked and bent, kicked and reared up, pulled back, rammed the bunk, twisted their heads, snorted, and foamed at the mouth. Simply put, they were quite put out! Safely out of sight in the haymow, I stood quietly and watched the battle with my knees shaking.

Leaving them to their misery, I exited the barn and returned an hour later, sneaking up to the feed trough from the opposite side, where I was able to unclip the ropes and turn them loose for the day. The next day, hunger overruled caution, and they inevitably returned to the trough, where I stealthily clipped a lead rope to each halter. Once again, they fought being captured, but this time to a lesser degree. By the end of the week they were used to the idea, and stood quietly. It was then that I untied their ropes and started training them to lead.

This, too, became a battle of wills—who was leading whom? Instinctively, an animal would try to run as I held onto the rope with all my strength.

Early on I painfully learned two cardinal rules of using hemp rope: wear leather gloves and do *not* loop the rope around a hand! Obviously, I was no match against the strength of the animal and I usually needed to enlist my dad's help. He tied the rope to the front of the tractor for a tug-o-war. When the tractor pulled back, the heifer pulled back in return. Occasionally a rope broke, allowing for a temporary escape. Eventually, the calf stopped fighting and succumbed to the idea of staying with me when I held the lead rope.

They were then ready to learn to walk and stand still in the show ring—another battle of wills, another tug-o-war. I'd pull with all my might and tugged with all my strength, but if that black heifer didn't want to move, it didn't move. Head down, front feet dug firmly into the ground, it pulled back when I pulled forward. Sometimes I needed help, and a quick-stepping assistant would slap the animal on the backside and jump away before the hind feet kicked out in response. My nephews, Dennis and Larry, usually came in handy about this time.

This long process was repeated several times over, for each heifer I planned to show. After weeks of sweat and frustration, my heifers and I finally worked as a team. We were ready for the big time—the county fair.

Show day was hectic and stressful as I groomed the heifers for the show ring. Their faces and the hair between the ears had been clipped with an electric shears before leaving home, so the first thing to do at the fair was shampoo the rest of the critters. That was an adventure, as they usually took an immediate dislike to the ice-cold water spraying from a garden hose, and I was always soaked before the task was completed.

Next I used a circular, sharply pointed currycomb to brush the wet hair away from the hide. I then turned the currycomb over to make "squiggles" that were brushed upward to create curls. Finally, I backcombed each tail into a fluffy ball and applied black boot polish to the hooves. Clipped, curled, and polished, the Black Angus heifers were finally ready for competition.

I will never forget the summer of 1963, following my graduation from high school—my final year in 4-H. In my crisp new blue jeans and starched white shirt with a cardboard entry number pinned on the back, I nervously held the leather lead rope of my best heifer with sweaty hands. The show calf walked proudly beside me, seeming to sense all eyes were upon her.

The casual observer would never know the amount of training and hard work that had lead up to that moment. Watching the judge in his Stetson hat, I directed my calf to hold her head high, walk calmly, line up and stand still. Using a long, thin show stick, I rubbed the calf's belly and nudged her feet to direct her into the proper foursquare position.

When the judge made his final decision and swatted my calf on the rump, I nearly burst with pride as I walked into the winners' circle with my heifer to accept the Reserve Grand Champion ribbon.

With the winning ribbon posted above the stall for fairgoers to view, the remainder of fair week was mine to enjoy. Tending to the cattle meant keeping them fed, watered, bedded, and comfortable. These tasks were completed quickly, leaving plenty of free time to enjoy the camaraderie of the East Boyer Rustlers 4-H Club and the other 4-H members who shared the cattle barn.

Some of my fondest memories of growing up in Iowa in the sixties revolve around showing 4-H calves at the Crawford County Fair every summer of my high school career.

Bonnie Ewoldt grew up on an Iowa farm and still enjoys county fairs and all things related to agriculture. She is a retired teacher and freelance writer with humorous and op-ed pieces published in national magazines, anthologies, and regional newspapers.

Photo provided by Karen Howard

ELEPHANTS NEVER FORGET

Karen Howard

"But I don't want to get up," I whined. Daddy was insistent and promised me a surprise. We were going on a big adventure, just the two of us. It was still dark outside and if my three-year-old self could have told time, I would have known it was 2:00 AM. I snuggled back under the covers and tried to go back to sleep.

Daddy persisted and I finally crawled out of the warm cocoon of my bed and got dressed in old play clothes and my favorite red coat. After a cold, dark ride to a less-than-savory part of Waterloo, we arrived at the train tracks in front of a stock rail car.

The surprise revealed itself when some smelly, dirty men lowered the gangplank and several elephants walked down onto the street right in front of me. I held Daddy's hand really tight as we watched the elephants being unloaded. Just like the pictures in my storybook, each was holding the tail of the elephant in front of it.

The smelly men led the elephants through the downtown area, to the National Dairy Cattle Congress grounds, where circus tents would be put up and where the elephants would perform that very afternoon. I didn't get to attend the matinee but I believe I got to see the best show in town that day.

Years later, when I was a bigger girl, it was a special treat when my parents would let us put on our pajamas, pop popcorn and pile into the car to go to the drive-in theater. I remember seeing *The Greatest Show on Earth*, a 1952 movie that starred Betty Hutton, Jimmy Stewart and Emmett Kelley. I must have been immensely impressed because the next day I was dangling from the rusty bars of the old swing set in the midst of a sand bur patch. I was the star of the trapeze, high above the middle ring, with prancing white stallions in one ring and gaudy ladies riding on the backs of the elephants in the other ring. It was a glorious sight, if only in the imagination of a nine year old girl.

And even many more years later, when my son was about three years old, he one day came running into the house, shouting, "There are elephants in the front yard!"

Like me, Rusty had a wonderful imagination, one shared with his friend John—whom only he could see. So naturally his daddy and I were slow to oblige him by going to the front window. Elephants simply do not cavort in the front yards of small town Iowa.

Imagine our surprise to see elephants really *were* in the front yard! A carnival semi with a stock trailer had cut the corner too short on the narrow asphalt road and the back wheels had slipped into the shallow ditch.

The three of us sat on the front stoop and watched as the carnies unloaded the elephants and harnessed them to the semi to pull it out of the ditch and back onto the road. When the elephants were reloaded, the truck headed down the road to set up the carnival tents at Meyers Lake, where they would perform that afternoon.

It all happened so long ago, but like an elephant I have not forgotten.

Karen Howard lives in Hartley, Iowa, with her dog Rose. She enjoys her family, reading, writing, quilting and working in her yard.

SEVENTY BELOW ON LAKE HERMAN

Bill Leonard

South Dakota winters are not for softies. The cold and snow that can paralyze an eastern city are standard for the Dakotas, where winter commonly begins near Thanksgiving and ends around Easter.

Thus, we Dakotans were pleasantly surprised when the balmy autumn of 1968 lingered into December. We knew it wouldn't last, but we couldn't have anticipated that reality would roar down on us with such vengeance.

Deep into the night of December 10, a winter that would be long remembered in all of eastern South Dakota staged its dramatic debut. The temperature plunged. The winds turned from zephyrs to screamers, pushing walls of snow into monster drifts. By morning the wind-chill was officially in the seventy-below range—the point at which numbers become meaningless.

At the time I lived alone in a small cabin on beautiful Lake Herman, four miles from Madison, in the southeast corner of the state. The half-dozen of us who lived on the lake and had jobs in town didn't make it to work that morning, or the next. The plows had more important roads to clear. They quickly fell behind in their work, and they stayed behind most of the winter.

My mailbox was totally buried in snow. When the first plow finally arrived, its blade found the box and ripped it away. I retrieved it and dug a pocket for it in the side of a drift, which became its home for the next three months.

Madison got 99 inches of snow that winter, and not an inch of it, which usually came with wicked winds, melted between storms. Some nights my neighbors and I who worked in town checked into the local hotel rather than risk the drive home. A well-used highway that passed a mile or so from our homes was kept reasonably clear through most of the winter, but when we turned off it onto the gravel shoreline drive, we were on our own. The marker for our turnoff point was the top few inches of a car that had been blown off the highway in mid-December and stayed buried until April.

One evening, with half a mile left and a tall new drift blocking my way, anger overcame good judgment. I bent over the steering wheel and pushed the gas pedal to the floorboards. My little VW bug surged, hit the drift, became airborne and made a four-point landing on the far side. Sheer luck.

The trials of the school bus drivers became legend. Time and again, as winter wore on, they called in from remote corners of the mostly-rural school district to report problems, receiving nothing but sympathy from a helpless dispatcher. All winter, students were warmed to dress very warmly—just in case.

An elderly farmer who lived far across the lake died sometime in January. It was three days before conditions allowed neighbors to deliver his body—strapped to a sled—to a mortuary in town.

My little cabin, built as a summer vacation getaway, was never intended to withstand a Dakota winter. The walls and roof were uninsulated, and the only warmth came from a dangerously overworked electric heater. Fortunately, the house had a huge fireplace, and, again fortunately, I had cut and stacked a huge pile of wood that fall. One bitterly cold night, as I crouched near the blazing fire, I heard a *snap* from the kitchen. My water pump, under the sink, had frozen and broke.

A plumber who was kind enough to come out a day or so later replaced the pump and showed me how to properly wind heat tape around the water pipes. My neighbor told me to bank snow up against the wall outside the kitchen for insulation. It worked for the rest of the winter.

Lake Herman is the westernmost of a series of glacial lakes, connected by a narrow and sometimes-dry ditch. It covers 1,000 acres, but drains eighty-one square miles of farmland. Sediment dumped by decades of erosion left the lake with a maximum depth of only ten feet. In the winter of 1968 – 69 it froze solid. Late in the winter, when wide cracks developed in the ice, the bodies of hundreds of dead fish were heaved to the surface.

Having arrived late, winter decided to stay late. Morning after April morning, Dakotans rose and gazed skyward, yearning for sunshine, tired to exhaustion by the endless weeks of gray. When winter's grip finally loosened, its departure was as abrupt—and, in a very different way, as dramatic—as its arrival.

On an April day, whose warmth and beauty are etched permanently in my memory, a burning sun washed the countryside. A timid trickle formed in the single stream that would drain the entire Lake Herman watershed, carrying runoff under a highway bridge and into the lake. Shyly at first, then wildly, the trickle became a torrent, bouncing and boiling under the bridge and into the lake.

It was Saturday. Word got around. In no time, cars packed the highway shoulders and half the countryside were standing on the highway bridge, smiling, joking, trading anecdotes from the winter they had finally outlasted, and gazing below as the warmth of life flowed joyously back into a long-frozen world.

Soon the meltwater had lifted the lake's 1,000-acre hunk of ice by more than a foot, leaving a fairly wide strip of open water along the shore. I pushed my old rowboat into the water and beckoned to a bunch of neighbor kids. They piled in, and I paddled along the shore next to the roadway as they waved and shouted. We whooped as if we were part of a Mardi Gras parade.

Hey—we'd earned it.

Bill Leonard is retired from a forty-three-year newspaper career that included papers in Nebraska, Kansas and South Dakota, and thirty years as an editorial writer for *The Des Moines Register*.

EAST MEETS MIDWEST

Brad Gray

We were sitting at the bar at Mary & Eldon's, just down the street from where we lived in Oxford, Iowa (pop. 705), drinking Rolling Rock beer at 50¢ a bottle. Behind the bar, Eldon was joking with his customers. He drew a circle with a stick outline of a tree underneath it on a piece of paper and pushed it over to me.

"Know what that is?" he asked. "That was the temperature at my house this morning—tree below zero." He burst into good-natured laughter over his own witticism.

Unlike the bars we were used to back in Boston, Mary & Eldon's was a family establishment. On this Saturday evening children rode tricycles up and down the linoleum floor, groups of four sat at tables playing euchre, and men sat at the bar discussing the relative hauling capacities of different models of John Deere vs. Allis-Chalmers tractors. A dozen pickup trucks were parked outside the tavern like so many horses tethered to the hitching rail in front of an old-west saloon. Unlike back home, the trucks were not locked; in fact, in most cases the keys were in the ignitions. When I asked one of my neighbors why he left his keys in the truck, he gave me a look of profound surprise.

"Why?" he repeated. "Well, because someone might need to borrow it!"

East meets Midwest, indeed.

In the summer of 1974, my wife and I had packed up our old Toyota station wagon and begun the 1,238 mile drive from Boston to Iowa City to start graduate school at the University of Iowa. With all our possessions crammed into the car or tied on the roof, we probably resembled another group of westward-bound migrants: Steinbeck's sharecroppers on their depression-era trek to California.

At the time, I don't think either of us had been farther west than Pennsylvania, except on transcontinental flights, which, of course, were not the same thing. To us, Iowa was a foreign land composed of idealized images conjured up by Grant Wood paintings: a benign landscape of rolling hills, small farms, corn fields, fruit trees, vegetable gardens and root cellars. Whether the natives would prove friendly or hostile, we knew not.

We picked up Interstate 80 just south of Wilkes-Barre, Pennsylvania and headed west, farther and farther into the American heartland, hour after hour, the miles clicking off on the car odometer: Ohio, Indiana, Illinois and finally, Iowa. What I remember most was the corn, miles and miles of green rows.

"What do they *do* with all of this corn!" my wife kept repeating.

Our first real encounter with the natives was at the Blue Top Motel in Coralville, just outside of Iowa City, where we were greeted by the proprietors with surprising (by eastern standards) warmth. The Blue Top was a 1950s-style motor court with nine individual small white cottages. (The motel has since been immortalized by *The Blue Top Motel*, a collection of stories about the establishment compiled by the second-generation owners.) From this snug base of operations we made forays into Iowa City in search of a place to live.

We soon found that the housing shortage in this university town of 25,000 students was acute. Every apartment, condo, duplex, townhouse or house seemed to be already taken, and some property owners were even renting out their garages to meet the need for student housing. To be sure, there were a few classified ads in the *Iowa City Press Citizen*, but even if we called an hour after the newspaper had hit the street, the answer always seemed to be the same: "Sorry, but it's already rented."

Eventually we struck up an acquaintance with one of the friendly natives who worked at the newspaper and who would leak us ads about apartment rentals before the paper had been published; but even with this "inside trader" information, we were getting nowhere.

The time had come to take stock of our dwindling resources. Even at $15 per night it was becoming clear we could not remain at the Blue Top indefinitely. Then we heard about the campgrounds at the Coralville Reservoir; no amenities but only $2 per night. The fee was so little, in fact, that some local families parked their campers there all summer and only used the site on weekends. Of course we didn't have a camper, only an older-model, four-person tent with a fly on the front, which became our new home.

We bathed in the lake and cooked meager meals on our two-burner Coleman camp stove. At night we tried to sleep through the Midwestern thunderstorms that frequently pounded the campground, peering apprehensively through the front flap of the tent as the lightning strikes lit up the radio tower on the other side of the dam. Being Easterners, we also listened warily on the car radio to reports about tornadoes—twenty-seven in Iowa that year compared to none in Massachusetts.

Finally, on one of our scouting expeditions to Iowa City in late August, our "Early Edition" friend at the newspaper fed us a somewhat unpromising-sounding lead that read something like this:

> House For Rent, Oxford, $100 per month.
> Call [phone number] or come to [address]
> and look for owner in trailer behind the house.

We were skeptical but we went anyway. School would be starting soon and, truth to tell, we were growing desperate. To our surprise and delight, the small, white gingerbread-style house on a quiet tree-lined street was actually quite charming. The owner, whose name was Jack, we later learned, was standing in the front yard talking with two long-haired, bearded students in bib overalls, and from the conversation we quite clearly caught the familiar words, "Already rented."

We turned to leave, but the owner raised his hand to stay us and we noticed that, with a twinkle in his eye, he'd winked at us.

After the students left, Jack explained the situation to us.

"This house belonged to my grandmother," he said, "and it's special to me. I come up from Arkansas for about a month every summer to do some repairs and stay in the camper out back. I need someone to look after the place the rest of the year and I don't want no hippies living here. You look like nice folks," he went on, "and if you'll do a little painting and just sort of look after things for me, I'll rent it to you for $100 a month."

We moved in the first week of September. By October we were settled in enough to find ourselves at Mary & Eldon's on a Saturday night with our new neighbors, taking a break from our academic studies at the university to play a little euchre and discuss the tractor pulling contest that had taken place that afternoon.

Brad Gray received his M. A. degree in English from the University of Iowa before embarking on a twenty-five year career as an acquisitions editor at Little, Brown, Butterworth-Heinemann, and several other nationally prominent publishing houses. Currently a freelance editor and writer working out of his home, he lives in a rural part of Massachusetts with his wife, Virginia, and a large Newfoundland dog, Siegfried.

CAMP PINNACLE AND THE PRUDE

Gary R. Hoffman

N one of us who worked at Camp Pinnacle near Buffalo, Missouri, were exactly sure what Monica's job was there. We all knew her father was friends with Chuck, the manager. Her father was also a minister and somewhat of a bigwig in the hierarchy of the United Church of Christ. Maybe Chuck, another minister in the UCC, knew the reason he hired Monica, but he never revealed it to any of us.

I was an assistant manager and lifeguard at the church sponsored camp. Jerry was another lifeguard and was also Chuck's son. Kathy, whose nickname was No-No, for reasons most people could only imagine, was a lifeguard and helped in the kitchen. And then there was Monica. She seemed to be doing things there, but no one could ever put a label on her job.

Monica was nineteen years old, but wore clothing that made her look like an old lady. She always wore long skirts and lace-up-the-front shoes, the heels of which were only about an inch high and were the kind many older women wore. Of course, they were black. She also kept her hair in a bun. Compared to No-No, who wore bikinis at the pool, it was difficult to imagine Monica as anything but a prude.

One of the minor perks of working at Camp Pinnacle was a night off once a week. This gave me and the other three permanent staff members a chance to get away from the camp and do something different. The town of Labelle was just twenty miles away, so we usually went there for the evening. There was a movie theater in Labelle, and the manager, being a good "church-goin' man," donated free passes to the staff of the camp for Wednesday nights. On an average Wednesday night, a total of ten people might attend the movie, so he probably felt he came out ahead because at least the camp people would buy popcorn and sodas.

After the show, we would usually go out to a truck stop on the highway and get something to eat besides camp food. The camp ran for ten weeks during the summer months and each week the menu was exactly the same, so any food that was different was a welcome change. On our way back to camp, in my car, we would usually try and find a diversion, like climbing an old fire tower, to delay our arrival back at camp.

On one such outing, our plans were made before we even left camp. Plans that included Jerry, No-No, and me. Monica would be going to the movie with us, but we just knew she'd never go along with the rest of what we had in mind, so we decided not to tell her.

The plan was to buy a bottle of liquor and take it back to camp with us. On our way out of town, we decided, I would make up some excuse to run into the drug store. Instead of just parking the car, Steve would ask if he could drive it around the block. While Steve was out driving, I would walk around the corner to the liquor store, buy some booze, and walk back to the front of the drugstore before Steve came back. When they picked me up, I would put my purchases in the trunk of the car.

Monica would be none the wiser.

We put our plan into motion. On our way back to camp from the truck stop I said, "Oh, shoot. I forgot something. I'm going to stop at this drug store."

As I started to pull into the parking lot, Steve spoke up. "Hey, how about letting me drive your car around the block while you're in there?"

"Yeah, I guess. Just be careful."

"Oh, I will be."

I got out of the car and started to go into the drug store. I stopped before getting there and acted like I was counting my money. As soon as the car was out of sight I walked quickly toward the liquor store. Once inside, I bought two pints of whiskey and a bag of chips. I insisted they each be put in separate bags. I was only twenty years old, but had been buying liquor without being carded for at least three years. I stuffed the two pints in my back pockets and carried the bag of chips.

Meanwhile, Steve was out driving around, trying to make it seem like he was getting lost so he could use up more time.

Finally he pulled up in front of the drug store where I was waiting. "Hey, toss me the keys so I can put this stuff in the trunk," I said. I caught the keys and went to the rear of the car. As soon as the trunk was open and blocking the view from inside the car, I deposited the bag of chips and the two bottles of booze. I closed the trunk and went back to drive the car home.

"We had room in the back seat for that stuff," Monica said.

"Well, it was just something personal," I said.

Monica just shrugged, and I drove away from the curb. At the end of the block I turned left. We drove right past the liquor store I had just been in.

"Hey, there's a liquor store," Monica yelled. "Let's stop and get some wine. I've got a fake ID, so I can go in and buy it for us."

Not such a prude after all.

Gary R. Hoffman has taught school, been self-employed, and traveled in a motor home. He has published or won prizes for more than 300 short stories, poems, and essays. Visit him on Facebook or at www.authorgaryhoffman.com.

Photo provided by Judy Olson

THE MAKING OF A MUSTANG ATHLETE

Judy K. Olson

My early athletic training involved the usual activities of a young child growing up on an Iowa farm in the 1940s—running, jumping and backyard games. But, being the oldest child in my family, and with my parents having had three children within two and a half years, I had younger siblings to coach, a job I took seriously.

We were a great team! Our favorite games were tag, kick-the-can, Mother may I? and Annie Annie over. When friends came to visit we tried pom-pom pull-away, drop-the-hankie, badminton, croquet and anything with a ball. Riding bikes, scooters, ponies and horses provided hours of fun.

We not only gained physical fitness with these activities, but we also used our creativity by making tree houses in the grove, and our imaginations in figuring out which games would be most fun in the creek or the barn. We also developed our problem-solving skills when we found the places behind the chicken house or cob shed we were least likely to be discovered smoking Dad's Camels.

After our noon meal I would suggest a game of badminton. Before our dinner was even settled we'd rush outdoors for fun while our parents had a little rest. I got some exercise and weight training from helping on the farm, but being smaller than my younger sister, and more of a literary type, the outdoor chores

131

went to her and my brothers, rather than to me. I was recruited to walk beans, cut thistles out of corn and to load bales onto the elevator.

Being full of energy, my motto was "Why walk when you can run?" I would often race through our house, jumping up to touch each archway along the way.

Once my siblings and I got into trouble for playing basketball in the living room, and breaking Mom's good lamp in the process. I have conveniently forgotten who was at fault for that accident.

Now, enough preparation for my athletic "success" in later years. On with the show . . .

Our school had a great tradition on the last day of school. The parents would all gather at noon, bringing with them ample baskets of food to share. I was always proud of my mother's offerings of fried chicken and rhubarb custard pie.

After the indoor picnic we headed outside to the school's track area for the events. Coaches and fathers organized the activities, which included the 100-yard dash, the high jump and standing broad jump, and four-person relay teams.

Many times I went home with a pocketful of coins from having placed first—50¢—or second—25¢—in an activity. Joan, Larry and I had practiced at home on the warm days of May before this event took place and it really paid off.

Now to explain the Mustang part of my story.

My school was located in Cleghorn and our mascot was the Mustang. In junior high we had organized basketball for both girls and boys, and played teams from the surrounding schools. I had grown to five-foot seven-inches by the time I was in sixth grade, a definite advantage, but I was self-conscious about being taller than anyone else in my class.

On one occasion when we played at nearby Marcus, the town my mother had graduated from, I became the designated free throw shooter for the night and scored nineteen points just from free throws. Dad was always our cheerleader and coach from the front row at midcourt, cheering or correcting, and giving directions or whatever he thought was needed at the time. But he did it in a good way, so I wasn't too embarrassed. He instilled in me a love of sports and a desire to do my best—probably way beyond my ability.

Then we began summer softball. We practiced on the school ball diamond by day and played the games there at night. We wore blue jeans and white blouses and white tennies.

Our coach was Francis "Smitty" Smith, who was the postmaster of Cleghorn at the time and, now in his nineties, is still going strong. Our small school of fifty-two students had organized softball and basketball for girls. I was especially happy about that because basketball was a love of mine.

As a freshman, I was the first sub on the basketball team and then I was on first team the rest of my high school years. Usually I was a forward, but I could play guard if my height and quickness were needed. At one hundred fifteen pounds, I carried no extra weight, which helped me move quickly on the court. Oh, to be skinny again!

Each year, when the Girl's State Basketball Tournament was held in Des Moines, the school board sent the first team plus the first sub, covering the cost of our hotel rooms and game tickets. We were there for the Thursday, Friday and Saturday games.

What fun we had! Besides watching the games, we walked several blocks to the state Capitol and climbed the stairs to the top of the dome. Our legs were very sore the next day.

Other pleasures were shopping, staying up all night talking, and playing card games. One year we thought it would be daring to fill water balloons and drop them from the seventh floor of the Brown Hotel. It wasn't so much fun when we were reprimanded for it.

Another year there was a blizzard that kept the Calumet girls from heading for home, as they'd planned. They hadn't kept their rooms for the night, so they slept on the floors in our rooms. It was a night of giggling and very little sleep.

During my high school years I also played softball, as a pitcher in rotation, right field and wherever else I was needed. We made it to the district tourney one year, where I came in as the second pitcher of the night. Almost right away I injured my little finger. It hurt badly, but I kept the pain to myself and finished the game. Sadly, we lost.

The next day my finger was swollen and I was in even greater pain. My mom took me to the doctor, where an X-ray showed a fractured bone. I wore a splint until it healed, and to this day I have a crooked little finger.

On to college sports.

I attended Morningside College from 1959 to 1963, on a teaching scholarship. No sports scholarships were given at that time and there were no teams for women's organized sports. That didn't stop us. Many of my friends in education had a love for basketball and had played in high school.

We formed a team, calling ourselves the Morning Glories. The head of the women's Physical Education Department was our coach, and we wore our burgundy one-piece PE uniforms— ugly! Informal games with teams from the business school, Westmar College and the St. Luke's nurses added to our enthusiasm for the game. Our team had some good players, and we often won.

Many of us from the basketball team also formed a drill team. We had permission to practice on the Allee Gym floor when it wasn't being used. We looked pretty cute in our short white corduroy skirts, maroon vests and white majorette boots. Our pom-poms were the same Maroon Chief colors.

We performed during halftime at the men's basketball home games. Years later the Morningside mascot changed from the Maroon Chiefs to the Mustangs so as not to offend Native Americans.

Early in my teaching career I was on a bowling team and later I played on volleyball and basketball teams at the YMCA. In my late thirties I also participated in a winter three-person marathon.

Yes, I have always loved to run!

In my mid sixties I injured a nerve in the ball of my foot by coming out of a winter of inactivity without the proper warm up, and going gung-ho on my running track. To hear my podiatrist tell me to limit my exercise for a few months while my foot healed was very discouraging, especially since I was planning my first trip abroad, to Norway and Sweden, for that summer.

So, now in my seventies, I try to be sensible, sticking to brisk walking and bike rides as my outdoor favorites. A large cemetery, with a quiet, hard-surfaced path, is adjacent to our backyard. I use that on nice days. On rainy or snowy days I dust off my two-pound weights, pedal the Air Dyne exercise bike or put on my Denise Austin exercise video.

I will continue to enjoy life, and plan to remain above ground in the cemetery behind my house. It's not time to put this old Mustang out to pasture yet!

Judy Olson, the oldest of four children, was raised on a Northwest Iowa farm. Born in the early 1940s, she experienced the effects of World War II during her childhood. She is married to Norm and the mother of two adult children, Julie and Mark. Now retired after thirty-six years as an elementary teacher, mostly in Spencer, Iowa, she has recently begun working on her memoirs.

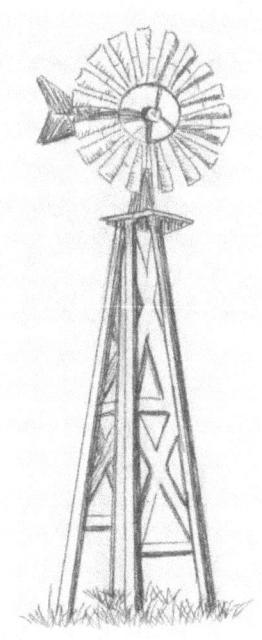

Photo provided by Steven Cutter

MOM'S BAKED ALASKA DISASTER

Steven Sebastian Cutter

My mother was the creative type, trapped in a tiny town in Wyoming. To use up some of that creative energy, and maybe also because her own mother—who died before I was born—didn't much like to cook, Mom was always trying out new recipes. Dad and I were her willing test subjects.

In the early 1960s, when a new show called *The French Chef* debuted on TV, my mother threw herself into improving her own cooking skills with enthusiasm, and Julia Child became a patron saint in our household. Most of the dishes were pretty good, even if Mom did tend to substitute ingredients. An early success was *Duck a L'Orange*, in spite of her having used frozen orange juice concentrate instead of orange liqueur, as the recipe called for. "Where am I going to find orange liqueur out here in the middle of nowhere?" she huffed. Another dish we liked was *Coq au Vin*, or chicken in red wine sauce, which also called for cognac. She didn't have cognac, so ignored the ingredient entirely, stating the red wine was enough booze for one main dish. She assured us the alcohol was cooked out of it in the oven, to which Dad, digging in, said, "Too bad."

There were a few failures, as well. Her crepes never did come out right, either so thick they would be better called pancakes or too thin to properly roll. The cheese quiche nearly put Dad in the hospital, and when she started muttering something that sounded like "Calf's brains in brown butter sauce" I fled to the barn.

Mom probably scored about an 80% success rate. For someone living nearly sixty miles from the nearest city, we considered that a pretty good average. When she tired of French cooking she picked up other new cookbooks. Dad gave her the *Better Homes and Gardens Cookbook*, with its red and white checked cover, for Christmas, and my Aunt Dorleen presented Mom with *The Joy of Cooking* for her birthday in June.

Most of all, my mother liked to experiment. So naturally Dad tried to talk her out of trying something new for the all-important event of having the new pastor of our church over. But this pastor had moved here from the city, and Mom was determined to make an impression. "I won't have him thinking we're a bunch of hicks," she declared, tying on her favorite apron and opening her *McCall's* magazine for ideas.

When she finally decided on a Baked Alaska for dessert. Dad groaned and left the kitchen, shaking his head.

On the evening of the visit, the pastor arrived with his mousy wife and their silent, twelve-year-old daughter. At fifteen I considered myself far above this child, and paid her little attention.

For the main course and the side dishes, Mom had agreed to stay within the safety-zone of meat and potatoes dishes, for which Dad was grateful. But dessert was to be her *piece de resistance.* She had prepared the separate parts of the baked Alaska ahead of time, as much as was possible, but during the main meal she kept jumping up from her chair to disappear into the kitchen to check on things. During her absences Dad kept things lively by engaging the pastor in various discussions about hunting, fishing and the merits of Ford over Chevrolet.

Mom returned. There was a dab of meringue on her cheek, which she wiped off with her napkin after Dad cleared his throat and discreetly touched his fingertip to his own cheek. The pastor looked amused, and his wife sweetly complimented my mother on the delicious pot roast. Their daughter remained silent.

We all heard the oven timer ding in the kitchen. Mom jumped up again. "That's the Baked Alaska!" she exclaimed, and disappeared into the other room.

"Oh, my," the pastor's wife said. "That sounds . . . ambitious."

Then we heard a wail of despair. No one moved. What were we going to do? Whatever was going on in the kitchen, we were all reasonably sure we wanted nothing to do with it. After what seemed a long time, the door to the kitchen swung open, and Mom appeared, her face red, hair working loose from her clips; her hands in oven mitts, she held a platter that supported what looked like a miniature Mount Vesuvius gone bad. Instead of being gently rounded with meringue, like in the pictures she had shown me, it peaked and leaned dangerously to one side, dark brown on one half, with a deep crater on top. Around the base was a melting goo that had to be the ice-cream interior.

"I'm not sure what happened," Mom said brightly, attempting to put on a brave face, as though we hadn't all heard the anguished scream of a few minutes earlier. "It's not very pretty, I'll admit that, but I'm sure it's still edible."

The pastor didn't look too sure, but his wife said, "I can't wait to try it."

Dad made room on the table for the platter and I set out the dessert plates. Mom, with her wedged pie cutter in hand, took a stab at the dessert. That only made things worse, as the meringue seemed to collapse into itself and more gooey ice cream oozed from the fissures. Mom's eyes began to blink rapidly. I wanted to do something to help, but felt paralyzed by uncertainty.

The pastor's wife rose to the rescue. She got up from her seat, picked up the oven mitts and the platter and herded Mom back into the kitchen. The rest of us sat in awkward silence for a few minutes, until Dad cleared his throat and started talking about the upcoming moose-hunting season.

We heard giggles from the kitchen, a sound almost as startling as the scream had been. The kitchen door opened again, and out came Mom and the pastor's wife. They carried with them a plate of store bought cookies and a pitcher of cold milk.

And so that was our dessert, that evening with the pastor's family—Oreo cookies and milk. Their daughter, whose name I finally learned was Jenny, smiled, showing a mouthful of metal braces, and joined in the conversation. Jenny and I cleared the table while our parents talked and laughed for another two hours.

Mom and the pastor's wife remained good friends for many years. Together they finally mastered the Baked Alaska.

Bon appétit!

Steven Sebastian Cutter has lived most of his life in Wyoming, where he does not fish or hunt but he enjoys cooking.

THE BLIND DATE

Rae Rogers

Growing up on tenant farms in northwest Iowa in the thirties and forties, I soon learned everything depended on the weather. With the biggest impact on the crops, weather ruled our livelihood, our moods, and our activities. The summer I was about fifteen, it also affected four teenagers' Saturday night plans.

There were only three families living on our mile-long graveled road. The neighbors across the road had a sixteen-year-old son, Dale, and a younger daughter; and I was my parents' third and last child. Dale and I were in the same class at Webb High School, but he was at least two years older—which meant he could legally drive!

Dale had, somehow, bought a second-hand convertible. On one particular Saturday night, he also had a visiting cousin, a boy about my age. Dale told me about his plans to take a new girlfriend to the show, and he asked if I would be his cousin's date. I quickly agreed, since my only other choice was to stay home with Mom and Dad and listen to the Saturday night radio shows. It was an easy decision.

The plan was that we would go to the movie theater at Sioux Rapids, thirteen miles away. With my parents' permission, I got ready for my date. I told them I would be home around nine-thirty at the latest.

Boy, was I ever wrong!

The closest I had ever been to riding in a convertible was in the rumble seat of my parents' 1934 tan coupe. That was no match for the excitement of being in a real convertible, and riding with the top down—but that wasn't to happen, either.

What really happened was that, after picking me up, Dale turned right, instead of left, at the end of our long lane and announced we were headed for Estherville to pick up his date. I had relatives there, so I knew Estherville was much farther away than little old Sioux Rapids.

The cousin and I found few things in common, so there was little conversation between us to fill the time. At last, Dale picked up his new friend and the four of us went to the second show at the theater in Estherville. I don't remember what we saw, or whether it was good or bad. But I do remember that when the show ended and we emerged from the theater, it was raining.

I was relieved when Dale parked outside the girl's house, where the porch light was shining brightly. But Dale evidently didn't understand the implication of that light. I knew what it meant. At my house, my parents turned on the outside light when it was time for me to go in.

Dale and his date sat in the front seat, talking. The rain was pouring down and the canvas top leaked rain all over the two of us in the backseat.

Still they sat . . . and sat . . . and sat.

Finally Dale walked his date to the door and stood . . . and stood, for what seemed like hours to his two drenched passengers.

In the meantime, I was really worried my parents might have stayed up until I was expected to be home. There was no way for me to let them know we were alright. We had no phone, and there would have been no way for me to call even if we had, because there was no phone at home, either.

Finally Dale came back to the car and we left Estherville. It was after midnight and still raining steadily, but at least we were on our way.

By the time we reached it, the long, barely-graveled lane leading to my house was like a river—and it was running full. Of course we got stuck!

There was no way to get out of our predicament without help. We had to get my dad out of bed to bring the tractor and to pull us out. By then it was three in the morning!

My parents were mostly just relieved that we were all safely home.

Not so Dale's Dad. The very next morning, as the sun came up, I saw Dale and his cousin out in the field next to Dale's house, tipping the oats shocks. I don't know if they'd been allowed any sleep at all.

A love of reading and two excellent English teachers first sparked **Rae Roger**'s interest in writing. Years later, as the youngest child of the youngest children, she recognized the need to pass on family stories and her own memories. And so it began . . .

A SWEET VACATION MEMORY

Richard Johnson

My little brother and I should have been sleeping soundly that night, early in August 1970.

But who can sleep when you're just ten and seven, and you and your family are leaving for a Black Hills vacation the next day?

Not us. If Mom had to wake us at all, we were instantly ready, hearts pumping, two skinny little sports-crazed boys who rarely sat still. We were all up early in the deep, hushed shadows of a lovely day—Mom, Dad, big sisters Lois and Sharon, Bob and I—packing our '68 Ford station wagon.

Mourning doves cooed as we gathered 'round our red car and "pop-up" Skamper trailer. Mom helped Dad back the car up to the camper hitch, and they made sure the signal lights worked. We climbed into the car, with Bob and me camped among our stuff at the far back, to begin the grand adventure.

Dad carefully backed us out of the driveway. I lay back in my comfortable berth and gazed up through the window to memorize a flash of greenery, the high-summer canvas of trees in our beloved neighborhood in Rochester, Minnesota, circa 1970.

It's a sweet memory: just us Johnsons, still together in my heart of hearts.

We made the long, non-air-conditioned trek west on Interstate 90, reading books, comics, newspapers and magazines, playing games, counting cows, bothering each other, eating lunch and playing catch at rustic country rest stops, following billboards toward the far-off Corn Palace, Wall Drug ("Free Ice-Water!" "See the Cowboy Orchestra Band!"), and the lumbering dinos at Dinosaur Park in Rapid City.

After camping the first two nights in Mitchell and then Chamberlain, South Dakota, we finally reached Sheridan Lake, our favorite spot in the scenic Black Hills.

For two weeks we swam in the ice-cold lake. We played catch, ate fried trout and SPAM. We had Zwieback toast, and Dad's great apple or SPAM pancakes. We enjoyed the rangers' nighttime nature programs in the scented deep woods, thrilled to wildlife—skunk in the campground!—ate more SPAM, and fell asleep to the sighing of the wind in tall Ponderosa pines just outside our camper door.

We pumped steely well water to brush our teeth, and grudgingly used those hellish, fly-and-Lord-knows-what-else-infested wooden "biffies."

We investigated Deadwood, home of Wild Bill Hickok, Calamity Jane, Crooked Nose Jack McCall, and all the other woolly Old West legends; Hill City and the surrounding area; and got covered with soot while riding the 1880 train at Keystone.

Back at Sheridan Lake we sat on beach towels amidst the smell of suntan lotion, and raced across the hot sand into freezing green water. Dad floated happily on his back, and a big trout leaped right over Sharon as she floated nearby. I dived to the bottom and hung there fetally, suspended in time and space. I screamed a happy underwater scream, the pressure of ancient depth throbbing in my ears. My young body sang with life.

Then, one early morning after breakfast, Mom and Dad hooked the camper back up and we turned east for the long, tedious trip home.

More books and comics. More rustic roadside lunches and family campgrounds with icky-tasting water. The bland, depressing smell of accumulating trash permeated the hot car.

I often relive the scene. I get excited when the scenery finally changed from drab, south-central South Dakota scrubland to the deep green of southern Minnesota.

We're at Worthington. Jackson. Fairmont. Blue Earth. Albert Lea. Austin. Dexter. High Forest. We're turning off Highway 90.

We're on Highway 63 North. We're back in Rochester, on the Beltline, rolling past the Dairy Queen and our old house on Fifth Avenue Southeast.

Hey, everybody! We're comin' home!

And then, by gosh, we're in our familiar neighborhood. We're turning onto Ninth Avenue.

We are in our good old gravel driveway. The house looks great. Don, our neighbor from across the street, strolls over to welcome us home, and my friends come running. Brian from down the street is dressed like an Indian. Bob and I do warwhoops and take off running with him and my best buddy Dave, four little Indian boys at home on the range.

Our house has a rather pleasant, buttoned-up-cottage smell. We get unpacked, eat supper, eat strawberries and ice cream, and watch TV 'til 10:30, safe and cozy back home, and still together.

Don died less than two months later. Ruby from next door followed early in '71. Bob and I and our friends grew up, went to high school, and moved on. It seems like it all happened in a flash.

Dad died in 2006. Mom lives in an independent living facility. Our old house has been empty for a few years. It and the garage are in disrepair. The grass goes unmowed. No one shovels the driveway in winter. Just a couple of neighbors are still left from my early years.

Upon returning to Rochester I often check on the old place, and half expect to catch a reflection of Dad waving hello from the picture window in our living room. He did love that house.

Perhaps someday we'll have another Johnson family vacation, in the heavenly Black Hills. The biffies have got to be nicer up there.

Get the Skamper ready, Dad. See you soon!

Richard Johnson was born and raised in Rochester, Minn. He's a freelance writer working for three beloved cats in Mason City, Iowa, just a stone's throw from the Black Hills. He keeps a fairly clean biffy and, incredibly, still enjoys SPAM.

Photo provided by Mark Walvatne

CIRCLE OF LIFE

Terry Overocker

Good eggs and bad eggs
Scrambled or fried
Done to perfection
Or crucified

Birds of a feather flock together
In all kinds of weather
Determined to fly
Needing to try

Life and death
First and last breath
Beginning to end
From start to finish survival depends

Desire and purpose
The will to go on
Choice and direction
The resolve to belong

Seasons of living
Oneness and strife
Taking and giving
The circle of life

Terry Overocker lives in a log cabin on the family farm where she grew up. She spends her time gardening and preserving most of the year's food. She also enjoys music, reading, writing, hiking and caring for her family of cats and a yellow Lab named Sammy.

THE END

OTHER BOOKS BY SHAPATO PUBLISHING:

Walking Beans Wasn't Something You Did With Your Dog: Stories of Growing Up in and Around Small Towns in the Midwest (2008)

Knee High by the Fourth of July: More Stories of Growing up in and Around Small Towns in the Midwest (2009)

Amber Waves of Grain: Third in the Series of Stories About Growing Up in and Around Small Towns in the Midwest (2010)

Make Hay While the Sun Shines: Fourth in the Series of Stories About Growing Up in and Around Small Towns in the Midwest (2011)

Horse Woman's Child: A Novel About Clashing Cultures on the American Frontier by Roger Stoner (2011)

The Earth Abides by Betty Taylor (2010)

Mama & Asha by Carolyn Rohrbaugh (2012)

No Turning Back: The South American Expedition of a Dragon Slayer by Benjamin "Coach" Wade (2011)

The Callie Stories by Karen Jones Schutt (2011)

Marcia's Life Application Bible: A Living Translation by Marcia Zubradt Cheevers (2012)

Turning Around the Heart: Stories of Possibility, Connection, and Transformation by Cindy Chicoine (2012)

SUBMIT YOUR STORY

The next Midwest anthology, tentatively titled *Needle in a Haystack*, is due for publication in late 2013.

If you'd like to submit a story for this or future anthologies, here are a few things to keep in mind:

- Send a true, original story of 600 – 1200 words.

- A Microsoft Word document as an email attachment is the preferred method, though submissions by mail –typed, please!—are also accepted.

- The deadline for each anthology is April 30th of the publication year.

- Photographs are welcome. A copy is preferred, but if you send an original it will be scanned and returned to you. Shapato Publishing accepts no responsibility for lost photographs, so be careful about sending those precious family photos.

- Payment for your story if accepted for publication is $10 upon signing of the contract, plus one free copy of the book when available.

Any of these details may change at any time. Nostalgia is always welcome, but so are contemporary stories if they fit in with the general theme of the anthologies, which is upbeat. Send to:

Email: jean@shapatopublishing.com

Mail: Jean Tennant
Shapato Publishing, LLC
PO Box 476
Everly, IA 51338